D0554820

ULI 92899

757575752

DATE DUE

GAYLORD			PRINTED IN U.S.A.

3 1215 00048 6347

On Criticizing Music

The Alvin and Fanny Blaustein Thalheimer Lectures
1978-79

Kingsley Price, editor

On Criticizing Music

FIVE PHILOSOPHICAL PERSPECTIVES

edited by

KINGSLEY PRICE

THE JOHNS HOPKINS UNIVERSITY PRESS

Baltimore and London

The Johns Hopkins University Press, Baltimore, Maryland 21218
The Johns Hopkins Press Ltd., London

Library of Congress Cataloging in Publication Data
Main entry under title:

On criticizing music.

(The Alvin and Fanny Blaustein Thalheimer lectures; 1978-1979
Includes bibliographic references.
Contents: Introduction / Kingsley Price—Influence,
plagiarism and inspiration / Charles Rosen—The state
of academic music criticism / Joseph Kerman—[etc.]
1. Musical criticism—Addresses, essays, lectures.
I. Price, Kingsley. II. Series: Alvin and Fanny
Blaustein Thalheimer lectures; 1978-1979.
ML3880.05   780'.1   81-47597
ISBN 0-8018-2613-6   AACR2

Contents

Contributors

KARL ASCHENBRENNER is the author of *The Concepts of Value: Foundations of Value Theory* (1971) and *The Concepts of Criticism* (1974), as well as translator with W. B. Holther of Alexander G. Baumgarten's *Reflections on Poetry* from the Latin, and with Donald Nicholl of Innocentius M. Bochenski's *Contemporary European Philosophy* from the German. He has contributed voluminously to learned journals in aesthetics and the history of philosophy. He is a composer and enthusiastic performer on the double bass, cello, and piano. He is Professor Emeritus in the Department of Philosophy, University of California, Berkeley.

MONROE C. BEARDSLEY is the author of *Aesthetics: Problems in the Philosophy of Criticism* (1958), *Aesthetics from Classical Greece to the Present: A Short History* (1966), *The Possibility of Criticism* (1970), and several other books that deal with aspects of philosophy quite different from aesthetics, editor of others still, and author of numerous articles in philosophical and related journals. He was President of the American Philosophical Association, Eastern Division, in 1978, and of the American Society for Aesthetics in 1967-68. He has held many other posts of responsibility in American academic life, and is Professor of Philosophy in the Department of Philosophy, Temple University.

JOSEPH KERMAN is the author of *Opera as Drama* (1956), *The Beethoven Quartets* (1979), and *The Music of William Byrd* (1980), as well as other books of musicology and numerous journal articles. He is editor of *19th-Century Music* and coeditor of *Beethoven Studies*. In 1972, he held the Heather Professorship of Music at Oxford University, and, in various years, has occupied other positions in music and the humanities in Great Britain and the United States. He is Professor of Music in the Department of Music, University of California, Berkeley.

CHARLES ROSEN is the author of *The Classical Style: Haydn, Mozart, Beethoven* (1972), *Arnold Schoenberg* (1975), *Sonata Forms* (1980), and many essays on musicology and the history of music. He is a frequent contributor to the *New York Review of Books* and the *New York Times*. Much of his time is devoted to piano concerts, to recording, and to lecturing on music. He holds a Ph.D. in French Literature and is Professor of Music in the Department of Music, SUNY at Stony Brook.

CONTRIBUTORS

ROSE ROSENGARD SUBOTNIK is the author of numerous articles on musicology and the history of music, especially of the nineteenth and twentieth centuries. In 1977-78 she held a fellowship from the American Council of Learned Societies, and in 1978-79 a Guggenheim fellowship. She is Assistant Professor of Music in the Department of Music, University of Chicago.

Preface

THE CHAPTERS IN THIS BOOK, except for the introduction, first saw the light of day as lectures delivered at The Johns Hopkins University in 1978-79. They constitute the sixth series of Thalheimer lectures. These lectures are made possible by a gift to the university from the Alvin and Fanny Blaustein Thalheimer Foundation.

Alvin Thalheimer (1894-1965) received the Ph.D. degree in philosophy from The Johns Hopkins University, taught philosophy there for a time, and then entered upon a career in business and energetic philanthropy. He devoted long and active service, especially to the Associated Jewish Charities, the Baltimore Council of Social Agencies, and the Maryland State Welfare Board. But throughout his life, he maintained his interest in things more strictly academic, publishing two books of philosophy and serving on committees at Harvard University and The Johns Hopkins University. His wife, Fanny Blaustein Thalheimer (1895-1957), attended Barnard College and The Maryland Institute, College of Art. She spent much of her time on charitable work, playing a particularly active role in the affairs of the Baltimore Museum of Art, the Peabody Institute, and the Maryland State Board of Education.

This sixth series of Thalheimer lectures, like the five that precede it, was presented by the Department of Philosophy of The Johns Hopkins University in memory of the public-spirited lives of Dr. and Mrs. Thalheimer. It recognizes in its theme—the nature of music criticism—the recent affiliation with the university of the Peabody Institute of Music.

My sincere thanks go to Professor Stephen Barker and Dean Michael Hooker, for help in organizing the lectures; to Dr. Elliot Galkin, director of the Peabody Institute, for excellent advice; to Margaret Yue and Nancy Thompson, for efficiently managing a great deal of correspondence; to Molly Mitchel, for preparation of a somewhat difficult manuscript; and to Brian Hall, for proofreading and many related tasks.

1

Introduction

KINGSLEY PRICE

UNTIL NOT VERY LONG AGO, from a historian's point of view, music led a distinctly dependent existence in the western world. It guided the dance, supported the declamation of poetry, and enhanced religious worship. Very early, there was composition for instruments alone; in 586 B.C., Sakadas won a prize for his composition for aulos at the Pythian games.[1] But the piece found its importance not in itself, not in its own character as an instrumental work, but in its representation of an episode quite different from music—the combat between Apollo and the dragon. Instrumental music, so far as we can tell, found its value in what it accomplished, not in what it was. And if antique shepherds piped in mountain meadows, they seem to have been charming away the ennui of tending placid sheep more than enjoying the beauty of their melodies.

Moreover, there is some evidence that music did not enjoy so high a reputation as did the activities it served. Plato derides musical amateurs as the last persons in the world to attend philosophical discussions, and as running about at Dionysiac festivals in town or country—"that makes no difference"—"as if they had let out their ears to hear every chorus."[2] And Aristotle writes, having excluded certain kinds of music from education altogether after Plato's example: "The right measure will be attained if students of music stop short of the arts which are practiced in professional contests, and do not seek to acquire those fantastic marvels of execution which are the fashion in such contests."[3] Music served needs more important and of greater prestige than the need to compose, to perform, and to listen to it.

The discussion of music in ancient and medieval times reflects its subservient position. Pythagoras (ca. 500 B.C.) developed a theory of acoustics that provided a remarkably good mathematical explanation of the characteristics of pitches in modes or scales. From him and his followers the theme of a mystical, mathematical identity between music and the cosmos evolved. Grammarians and musicians cataloged rhythms and meters. They considered how they should and should not be combined with one another, and with melody, but always in the light of the kinds of emotion and character that the rhythms and the melodies expressed, and of the meanings carried in the dance performed, the poetry declaimed, the worship participated in, and the story told. Music was discussed because of its relations to other things; there seems to have been little or no criticism of particular compositions—of their character or of their performance. How should it have been otherwise? Music, if pervasive of human life, was nonetheless an ancillary art.

This was its condition as one of the seven liberal arts, the major curriculum of general education through the Middle Ages; but in recent centuries, music has assumed another role. We still hear it, of course, in the ballet, the opera, and the Mass. But now, we also listen, in the public hall and private living room, to it, itself, and for itself alone. Music no longer needs something else: a dance to guide, a poem to clarify, an act of worship to enhance, a program to represent. It is an independent art, and shows a value of its own.

This new-found independence raises questions about music different from those previously asked. Of course, not wholly different. Its physical basis still commands attention; and the Pythagorean explanation still holds, although now supplemented by modern physics, neurology, and psychology, and though the identity it put forward between music and the cosmos receives less frequent celebration. But when the importance of particular compositions was found outside themselves in their effects on nonmusical activities or in what they represented, questions about them that now seem paramount could hardly have arisen. When compositions of music were not important in themselves, neither were their origins; and few questions, if any, seem to have been asked about them. But now that these compositions have value in themselves, their genesis is of great interest, and the history of music, a major aspect of literature dealing with the art. Nor, when there was little interest in compositions for themselves, did one discuss details of internal structure and how they fit together to form a whole; but now, when criticism would advance understanding and appreciation of particular compositions, it must show what those compositions are by setting out the configuration of their musical components. When compositions always carried dance or poetry or worship or programs with them, they had a meaning, and what that meaning was, was evident. There was no need to ask about it. But now that they are separated from these other things and valued for themselves alone, whether they have meaning and, if so, what it is, are topics of puzzled and absorbing interest. We feel that they must mean something still; yet it seems they cannot, since they contain no gestures, no verses, no religious yearnings, no programmatic significations.

The modern separation of music from dance, poetry, religion, and story, and the valuing of it for itself alone have led to three questions about any composition: 'what is its genesis?' 'what sort of thing or structure is it?' and 'what is its meaning?' The answer to the first presents a composition as a product in some strand of causes and effects; to the second, as a set of musical items configured in a certain structure; to the third, as a sign of a certain kind that carries a certain signification.

Monroe C. Beardsley, in this volume, points out that these answers embody different ways of understanding a piece of music—what he calls the "genetic," the "configurational," and the "semantic."[4] Now criticism of music is the effort to understand and to appreciate compositions for oneself, and to further their informed appreciation in others. Each of the following essays deals, in one way or another, with criticism; and in doing so, with one or another of these ways of understanding a composition.

One phase of the genetic development of music is its response to, and its thrust against, extramusical processes. There are fewer oratorios written when religious authority diminishes, and when jazz spreads across the globe, the manufacture of transistor radios increases. But in another phase, the development of music is internal to the art. This development is the influence of earlier upon later composers. This influence flows through the acquaintance of one composer with the works of others, and the historian traces it by observing similarities between the elements of later and earlier works, and by inferring the influence of the earlier upon the later.

For Charles Rosen, criticism of a composition combines a historical account of the influence of earlier compositions upon it with analysis of it. It aims, in Beardsley's words, at an understanding that is both genetic and configurational. But in his essay in this volume, "Influence: Plagiarism and Inspiration," Rosen writes primarily about influence. He considers how it can be discovered where the historian-critic studies compositions only, i.e., where he can look for evidence of influence (and this is the critic's usual situation) only to a comparison between the composition that interests him and the work of earlier composers. Rosen suggests a standard for the justification of belief in influence, mentions several kinds of resemblance of importance for the historian and critic, and arrives at an interesting conclusion about the role of genetic understanding in criticism of original compositions.

The influence of one composer on another falls on a scale that runs from plagiarism to inspiration. As in the other arts, plagiarism occurs in music where one artist puts into his work an important element that he takes from the work of some other and gives this element no transformation whatsoever. The element must be important. A trivial resemblance does not make for plagiarism. But an important identity with an earlier work, the historian cannot regard as fortuitous, and he attributes the later work to influence of the earlier without hesitation. Inspiration occurs where, though one artist takes an element in his own work from that of another, he transforms it so thoroughly that his work is original nonetheless. Finding no important resemblance between the later and the earlier work, the historian can support no claim for influence though he may feel certain of its presence. Plagiarism is ample evidence for influence; inspiration is none at all even though influence may be present.

Between plagiarism and inspiration lie differing degrees of resemblance. As the resemblance between a later and an earlier work diminishes, the justification for belief in influence diminishes also. And where the resemblance disappears, i.e., where inspiration thoroughly transforms the borrowed element, so also does the warrant for belief in influence. So, the standard for justification of belief in influence is the degree of resemblance between elements in the later and earlier compositions. The greater the resemblance, the stronger the assurance of influence; the smaller the resemblance, the weaker.

Rosen points to three important kinds of resemblance that serve as evidence for influence. One is rhythmic, like the resemblance between Mozart's Gigue for Piano

(K. 574), bars 5-8, and the finale of Haydn's Quartet in C Major op. 20, no. 2, bars 83-87. Another is primarily tonal—resemblance of themes and of their development; this is a resemblance any listener may recognize. The third is resemblance of structure like the resemblance between the finale of Brahms's Piano Concerto no. 1 in D Minor and the last movement of Beethoven's Piano Concerto no. 3 in C Minor—a resemblance accessible only to the connoisseur. Resemblance of the first two kinds is the resemblance of materials in the compositions. Resemblance of the third kind involves no important resemblance of material; what is borrowed is the structure of the earlier composition. The later composer takes the structure of the earlier composer's work as a model for his own—as a form into which to pour his own rhythmic and tonal material. Still, the degree of structural resemblance determines the degree of justification for belief in the influence inferred. The greater the resemblance, the greater the justification; the less, the less.

Rosen holds that some composers who are influenced do more than borrow, merely. In his Piano Sonata in C Major op. 1, Brahms not only borrows from Beethoven's "Hammerklavier"; he also refers to it. And in his Piano Concerto no. 2 in B-flat Major, he not only borrows from, and refers to Beethoven's *Emperor* Concerto, but also makes an important assertion about the relation between that concerto and his own.

The historian-critic is interested in tracing influence—in studying sources as Rosen puts it. Where his study of a composition can succeed, there are important resemblances that show the channel through which influence flows toward the composition. But the works in which he is often most interested are those that are highly original, and these are, precisely, those in which borrowed elements are so transformed that no important resemblance relates them to their predecessors. The inspiration of originality leaves no telltale marks. And short of some external evidence, such as a composer's statement that he has borrowed from another (a rare occurrence), the history of the most original compositions cannot be written. Here the critic's study of sources cannot come to fruition, and here, where most is at stake, the critic's genetic understanding must leave the field wholly to analysis. Often the critic may further comprehension of a composition by finding evidence for its development under the influence of earlier works; but where this influence cannot be evidenced, where the influence is inspiration, he must resort for understanding to a description of the composition's configuration.

Rosen documents his points about resemblance with quotations from compositions that exemplify them. One who reads music notation with ease will see in these examples an illuminating and lively support of the English text. One who does not may hear the same support by playing a phonograph. All the compositions to which Rosen refers are readily available on records.

The analysis or configurational understanding for which genetic understanding must sometimes make room, in Rosen's view, is the chief topic of Joseph Kerman's essay, "The State of Academic Music Criticism." Analysis can be understood, he holds, only in terms of its subject matter. This is the literature of the great Austro-German tradition of composition, extended through Schoenburg and the other serialist composers.

Although this tradition comprises very different styles, the compositions in it are characterized by a single trait—organicism or the coherence of their elements. In the earlier stages, from Bach through Brahms, Wagner, and Strauss, compositions take pitches for their elements, and, for the coherence of these elements, the relations they bear to one another that flow from hearing pitches as tones in scales—the relations of demanding, implying, and requiring that one tone sustains to others. Schoenburg, before World War I, added motives, rhythms, and textures to the elements of music; and to their coherence, the relationships to one another in which terms of these kinds can stand—relations that differ markedly from those of tonality. After World War I and into the fifties, Schoenburg and other serialist composers returned to pitches as the chief elements of music. However, they found its coherence not in relations of tonality, which they had rejected, but in the rules they had adopted for their writing. From Bach through the serialist composers, the Austro-German tradition gives us compositions in which the elements are held together in an organic way, though earlier this organicism is that of tonality while later it is that of rules deliberately adopted on the basis of a perception more intellectual than aural.

Impressed with the greatness of this tradition, critics have come to think of it as definitive of all music. A composition, they seem to hold, must be pitches in organic relations to each other. To analyze it, to come to understand it and to help others toward understanding it, therefore, is to work toward perceiving it as a configuration of pitches. Analysis "sets out," Kerman writes, "to discern and demonstrate the function and coherence of individual works of art, or, as is often said, their organic unity."[5]

But analysis does not try to understand a piece of music by noting all the relations of all its pitches. That would be impossible. Rather, it looks for a configuration of central terms in which all the others find their place. Tovey understands compositions as sequences of pitches that fill up forms based on relations of the tonalities of its major sections, and Schenker (see examples 1 and 2 in Kerman's essay) sees them as sequences that fill up some arpeggiation of the tonic triad. Analysis—as the effort to show how the pitches in a given work do or do not fill out a form or an arpeggiated tonic triad, do or do not fit into an organic unity derived from the serialist's rules—dominates the criticism of music in the American academy or university. Kerman holds that analysis, especially Schenkerian analysis, cannot find important aspects of a great deal of music, it must be supplemented with other ways of understanding if criticism is to perform its proper function—the furtherance of the understanding and appreciation of music.

Kerman's argument is the consideration of a particular case—Robert Schumann's "Aus meinen Thränen spriessen" from *Dichterliebe* op. 48 (example 1 of his essay). Schenker analyzes this famous song as a filling-out of the A-major triad, arpeggiated from the median through the supertonic to the tonic (example 2). Kerman insists that this understanding of the song directs attention away from its most important and distinctive features. These features are or include the song's relation to the genre of the nineteenth-century German lied with its emphasis on popular folkways, the connection between its music and the music of the song that precedes it in the cycle, the connection between its words and the words of that preceding song, its combination of musical and verbal elements—of chromaticism with certain words, especially *klingen*, musical symbols of Clara Schumann, its character as a joint activity of two persons—one who sings and one who plays, and above all, the cadences paired for voice and piano with their accompanying fermatas at the end of line 2, line 4, and line 8 of Heine's poem.

Now, none of these traits can be conceived as filling out the arpeggiated triad that Schenker refers to. Only pitches can be found between the tones that make that chord. But the relation between a song and a genre, between the music of one and that of another, and between the words of one and those of the other; the whole formed of music and words, musical symbols, joint activities, the pairing of cadences—none of these is a pitch, or a property of a pitch alone, and none can fill out the spaces between the tones of a triad. Consequently, the Schenkerian analysis of the song cannot bring before the mind its most important and distinctive features. Kerman extends his conclusion to all analysis. He holds that analysis is not mistaken in the understanding it provides, but insists that that understanding cannot be the full comprehension of a great many compositions.

The outcome of Kerman's essay is not that the American academy should reject analysis. On the contrary, it should retain analysis as one way of understanding music. But it should add to analysis such other procedures as are required to bring before the mind important features of musical compositions that it misses. Robert Morgan holds that analysis should be made to include an examination of what the composer intends to realize in his composition, the way in which his system implies it, its relation to older as well as present-day music, the perceptual problems it involves—indeed, everything, apparently, that might add in any way to understanding the composition. Kerman quotes Morgan with approval, and recommends this greatly enlarged enterprise to the American music academy, adding that although the academy may find the new procedures perplexing, the rest of us will not if we recognize the enterprise as criticism rather than analysis only. The American academy is right in supposing that the listener's comprehension is enhanced by a description of the composition's configuration. But the configuration the critic should describe is that of many kinds of elements internal to the composition, not of pitches only; and it includes, as well, the configuration of the composition with other terms in the indefinitely extendable context in which history has placed it.

Monroe C. Beardsley, in his essay, "Understanding Music," points to the three ways of understanding that we have already noticed. He holds that it is obvious that a composition of music may be understood in the first two, and puts forward an argument for the possibility of understanding it in the third.

The first way of understanding Beardsley calls "genetic." It consists in knowing the conditions that make an object what it is. In this way, the historian and critic understands a composition when he knows the events, social, psychological, etc., that usher it in, and determine its character. Rosen describes one phase of this kind of understanding, and notices where it cannot succeed in advancing the critic's own, or his readers', comprehension. The second way of understanding is "configurational." It consists in knowing how the elements of an object "fit into a pattern or structure that characterizes the whole." In this way, the music analyst or critic understands the composition by making evident to himself and others its details in their relation to each other. Kerman describes one phase of this kind of understanding, and suggests a supplement for it. The third way of understanding, the "semantic," "consists in knowing what something signifies." It is evident that nothing can be understood semantically unless it is a sign, and Beardsley's primary concern is to show that a composition of music is one.

If a composition is a sign, it refers to something; and since nothing can refer to something in the absence of a rule that makes it do so, there must be a rule (perhaps a set of rules) that tells us what a musical composition refers to if it is a sign. Beardsley looks for such a rule.

In his search for it, he notices that some criticism describes compositions with the help of words for qualities like those of human life—qualities that are emotional and psychological. It may describe a composition as ironic or angelic. Other criticism describes compositions in a perfectly neutral way, holding that if they involve human qualities, they are the qualities of emotions and states that they evoke, not of the compositions themselves. It may describe a composition as putting its listeners in an ironic or angelic frame of mind. Beardsley holds that criticism of the first kind is more adequate than the second. Compositions do really possess human qualities. And his theory of the semantic aspect of compositions is that they refer to such qualities.

Before explaining this theory, Beardsley considers five others. Wilson Coker holds that compositions refer to emotions, and he bases this assertion on a general theory of signs. This theory has two forms: first, one thing is a sign for another if an organism behaves in its presence in a manner appropriate to the other; secondly, one thing is a sign of another if and only if it accompanies, follows, or refers back to the other.[6] The application of this theory to compositions shows that it cannot be true. Though the passacaglia theme in the slow movement of Bach's Keyboard Concerto in D Major should be a sign for spiritual travail, we cannot suppose that the listener (the organism) therefore endeavors to assuage some person's misery. Nor can we suppose that there is some spiritual travail that the theme always accompanies, follows, or refers back to; the listener is not always in travail simultaneously with or before its occurrence. The general theory of signs to which Coker gives his allegiance is not true. And, of course, even if it were, it could not support Coker's view that compositions are signs; it could only tell us why they are so if they are so.

Deryck Cooke holds that compositions refer to human qualities. He draws this conclusion from the fact, abundantly supported, that many of the figures they contain possess them. He assumes, unknowingly, that possession of a quality proves reference to it; and consequently, he brings forward no rule for its reference.

Beardsley holds that Donald N. Ferguson makes the same assumption more explicitly, and that he develops it as follows. An emotion shows three constituents: the object (its "contextual concept") upon which it is directed, Juliet for example; a certain tension, Romeo's longing; and a certain motor activity, his climbing the balcony. It is the "contextual concept" that distinguishes one emotion from another, not the tension and activity—Juliet that distinguishes Romeo's love from hatred, not his longing or climbing. A composition possesses tension and activity, and it induces the listener, Ferguson holds, to think of the contextual concept. The difficulty is that Ferguson adduces no rule that enables this thought; so that no emotion can be referred to because none in particular is.

Gordon Epperson, according to Beardsley, tries another path to the conclusion reached by Cooke and Ferguson. A composition frees the essence of an emotion from its particular embodiment and sets it out altogether clear to the listener's aural view. But essences symbolize what they are essential to, and a composition symbolizes the motion whose essence it sets forth. Again, Epperson brings us no rule that enables an essence to refer to its particulars.

Beardsley finds more help in a fifth theory. Nelson Goodman maintains, as do Cooke, Ferguson, and Epperson, that a composition of music is a sign; but he does not hold, as they do, that it is a sign for something quite other than itself—an emotion or a psychological state. Rather, it is a sign for some of its own properties.

Predicates refer to (denote) the things they are predicated of; "is blue" denotes Jones's blue car as well as every other blue thing. "Now," Beardsley writes expounding Goodman's theory, "suppose that Jones's car *also* refers to the predicate that denotes it; then Jones's car exemplifies that predicate. . . . Goodman . . . reluctantly allows a more comfortable idiom in which it is properties . . . that are exemplified."[7] A double reference of property to thing and of thing to property makes the thing exemplify the property as a painter's color sample exemplifies its color. Works of art, in general and, therefore, compositions of music, exemplify some of their qualities. The irony of a composition denotes the composition, and the composition refers to the irony. And the composition, in this way, signifies the human qualities that it possesses.

Beardsley agrees that compositions signify their qualities by exemplifying them, but he holds that Goodman's explanation of their semantic character is incomplete. They can exemplify or display their properties, Beardsley holds, if and only if they themselves are displayed or referred to; a sonata can exemplify and refer to its properties if and only if someone refers to it by performing it. Goodman does not notice that exemplification presupposes an independent reference to the example. But the more conspicuous deficiency in Goodman's theory lies in its inability to explain why a composition exemplifies some but not all of its properties. This inability amounts to a failure to bring forward a rule that gives a composition its reference, and Goodman's theory swells the company of those that claim significance for music but do not provide the chief condition for it.

Beardsley supplies this condition. A composition does not exemplify its key; 'being in that key' is a property of no aesthetic interest. But it does exemplify such properties as 'unusually diffident,' 'hesitant,' and 'indecisive.' Consider the first movement of the Piano Sonata op. 101 of Beethoven. But these properties are of aesthetic importance. A composition is a sign for some of its properties, and the rule that Beardsley supplies for distinguishing them from those it does not exemplify is this: A composition exemplifies those of its properties that are of aesthetic importance. These are its human qualities. Thus, for Beardsley, we may understand compositions of music in the semantic way, because they are signs for their human qualities.

Beardsley notices that many of the human qualities a composition signifies are characteristics it shares with other things. Most important among these is what he calls "continuation." A composition continues through time from beginning to end; and in that continuation, it shows development or retrogression, decisiveness or doubt, determination or hesitancy, building or disintegration. This continuation with its numerous species is also a characteristic of human experience generally. For that reason, Beardsley describes it, together with its species, as metaphysical.

The metaphysical traits of a composition, because they are shared with aspects of life that are moving, make compositions move us as do the things they resemble. And because of these shared traits, as well as the fine discriminations between kinds of continuation that music exhibits, compositions may be instructive. They may be used as models for human experience in its many aspects.

Beardsley draws a surprising conclusion from his theory of the semantic aspect of a composition. It is that the semantic understanding of it can play no role in the criticism of it. Criticism must further the understanding and appreciation of a composition; and an essential part of this task, the part that pertains to understanding, consists in bringing the composition clearly before the mind—the composition with all its important qualities, including those that are aesthetically important. But understanding a composition semantically consists in using it as a whole, with all its qualities, to exemplify just those aesthetically important qualities, so that semantic understanding cannot occur until after the composition, with all its important qualities, has been subjected to criticism. Semantic understanding may follow after criticism; but it can play no part in criticism, itself. This exclusion means that criticism must be either genetic or configurational.

In her essay, Rose Rosengard Subotnik adopts the view that in its effort to promote understanding and appreciation of music, criticism directs attention to its meaningfulness. Her view on the subject of meaning differs from Beardsley's. She holds that meaningfulness is of two kinds. A thing is meaningful if it bears a certain relation to something else that is meaningful; but it is also meaningful if it bears a certain relation to something that is not meaningful at all—at least, not in its own language. A thing is "semiotic" (her word) if it is meaningful in either or both of these ways.

But Subotnik's primary concern is not so much the nature of music criticism as the distinction between criticism of classical and of romantic compositions. She formulates this distinction by reference to differences in the meaningfulness attached to compositions of each kind, and to the different capacities (she calls them "competences") required for perceiving, and for helping others to perceive these differences.

The meaning of classical compositions is of the first kind mentioned above—a certain relation that one sign bears to others. Those not acquainted with music are most familiar with this relation in the sentences and paragraphs of language. If a sentence is meaningful, its words must be related as adverb to verb, subject to verb, etc.; and if a structure of sentences is meaningful, its parts must be related in certain ways, for example, as premises to conclusion. A collection of words or sentences whose parts bore to one another no such relations would be meaningless. Of course, their presence does not provide complete meaningfulness; a sentence in which we could recognize a subject and a verb, but a subject and a verb that had, for us, no reference to things outside their home language, must be only partially meaningful.

Still, what meaning it has is provided for it by the relations that its parts bear to one another. Subotnik describes semiotic structures, insofar as their parts are related in this way, as syntactical or logical; and it is this syntactical meaningfulness that characterizes classical compositions.

We must dwell a little on the semiotic character (syntax) of classical compositions. The relations between their parts resemble the relations between the parts of a linguistic structure. It is in the nature of a subject to require a verb, and a verb a subject. "He" must be accompanied by something like "jumps," not just by something like "quickly"; and "jumps" by something like "he," not just by something like "speaks." "He jumps" is meaningful; but "he quickly" and "speaks jumps" are not.

Analogously, it is in the nature of one tone to require a certain other—of the seventh, for example, to require the eighth, and of the fourth to require the third; and consequently, of one chord to require a certain other chord—of the dominant seventh to require the tonic triad. A sequence constituted by the dominant seventh followed by the tonic triad is meaningful by virtue of the requirements inherent in the tones involved. Since the elements of classical compositions are tones in scales and chords made of them, the meaningfulness of those compositions is the fact that each element is required by the very nature of some other. The meaningfulness of a composition by Haydn or Mozart (the meaningfulness of a work by Beethoven would not serve so well), though it attaches to a much larger structure, is like the meaningfulness of "he jumps." A structure whose elements are tones or chords, but such that those that are required by some are, nonetheless, not present, is not meaningful. Its meaninglessness is like that of the linguistic structure, "he quickly" and "speaks jumps." The syntax of classical compositions is the meaningfulness yielded by the tonality of their elements.

But this description does not make quite clear the meaningfulness peculiar to classical compositions. Tonal relations bind their elements together into sequences that are melodic, harmonic, or contrapuntal; and such sequences are meaningful in themselves. Now a classical composition is a sequence of such sequences; but such a sequence of them that in it, sequences that are earlier require those that are later. So, in the sonata, the first theme in the exposition finds its meaning in the tonal relations of its elements; while by virtue of that meaning, the first theme requires the second. And by virtue of its meaning, the exposition requires the development; the development, the recapitulation; etc. The meaningfulness of a classical composition attaches to the entire composition, and consists in the tonal relations of the sequences that constitute it.

This meaning is widely accessible. Every normal person can hear the relations of dominant to tonic, of theme to bridge, of exposition to development, etc.; just as he can perceive the relation between the rose and its color, the fire and the burning of the paper put into it. Kant held that the rose must necessarily have a color, and that the fire must necessarily burn the paper because of the way in which experience is organized. Now, it is we who organize it, and since our ways of organizing include putting qualities on substances and causes with effects, every substance, and therefore the rose, must necessarily have a quality, its color, and every event, and therefore the fire, must necessarily have an effect, the burning. The necessary connection between substance and quality, cause and effect, is accessible to all because each person puts things together in those ways. Indeed, all the relations that things must necessarily bear to one another yield structures that reflect structures in the minds that experience them.

Subotnik stresses the analogy between perceiving substances and causes, and hearing classical compositions. One who listens hears the earlier sequences of a Haydn or Mozart piece requiring later sequences; and this "requiring" is very like the necessity with which a substance is related to its quality, and a cause to its effect. If he were to explain this musical necessity, Kant might say that we organize pitches in such a way that one requires another, that one chord or sequence requires another, etc. So that just as the structure of an experience of things has a meaning that depends upon our having put things in that structure, so the structure of a musical experience depends upon our having put pitches in that structure. And the universal accessibility of the semiosis of classical compositions is established by the fact that each listener, in organizing them, gives to them, from out of his mind, the meaning-fulness he finds them to possess.

Romantic compositions have a meaninfulness that differs markedly from that of classical compositions. The meaning of a classical composition pervades the entire composition, and depends only on the principles of tonality. But the meaning that tonality provides for a romantic composition attaches only to constituent sequences. In Chopin's Prelude in A Minor, for example, there are three chief sequences —"bars 1-7, 8-12, and 13 to the end"—and each secures its meaning from tonal principles. But each is, with respect to its tonality, quite unconnected with the other two; so that the meaning of the entire composition, if it has one, cannot be its tonal structure.

But the entire prelude does have a syntactical meaning. It is not provided by tonality as is the syntax of a classical composition. Tonality makes the elements within sequences mean one another; and through its derivative, harmony, provides color for constituent sequences. But the syntactical meaning of the whole romantic work consists in cyclical recurrence, thematic resemblance, and rise and fall of pitch level. And besides this difference in syntactical meaning, the whole work carries another kind of meaning that differs radically from that of a classical composition. It means something not itself a sign, and quite outside its language—the language of music. It means the entire set of twenty-four preludes of which it is one, the pos-sibilities of different keys that they explore, Bach's similar enterprise, and the nature and emotional qualities of death.

The semiosis of any romantic composition is like that of Chopin's prelude. Each sequence within it carries syntactical meaning provided by tonality; but as a whole, it shows no syntactical meaning stemming from that source. Instead, the syntax of the whole is provided by other principles. To the syntactical meaning of the whole, a romantic composition adds a semantic meaning that gives it reference to things quite different from the composition that is meaningful—to things that are suggested by titles, texts, and programs, and as with Mahler's First Symphony, to preexisting musical compositions. The semiosis of classical compositions is the syntax that pervades each work, attaches to the whole, and springs from tonality. The semiosis of romantic compositions is the syntactical meaning of subordinate sequences that springs from tonality, the syntactical meaning of the whole that springs from non-tonal sources, and the semantic meaning of things quite distinct from the composition.

Subotnik views romanticism as a challenge to the Kantian account of the meaningfulness of music. This account regards the syntactical meaning of music as consisting in relations of tonality understood as binding together all the sequences of a composition, but romantic compositions show a syntax based on nontonal relations. The Kantian account regards syntactical meaning as the reflection of a priori mental principles of organization; but romantic compositions, as wholes, are often organized by principles learned from experience — the experience of the style of their composers, of particular musical forms, or even of the very composition they organize. If learned from experience, the principles that give syntactical meaning cannot be a priori and mental. The Kantian account holds that the meaning of musical compositions is the same in all; but romantic compositions often carry highly individualized, semantic meanings that can be found in no other. And romantic music is the criticism of Kantianism that it cannot possibly be true for music generally taken.

Subotnik draws a conclusion concerning what is required for criticism of classical or romantic music. Music criticism makes clear the semiotic character of its subject. In classical compositions, this character is found in the tonal relations that relate pitches in sequences, and sequences in entire compositions. The criticism of classical compositions requires, chiefly, the capacity for discriminating perception of tonality. Subotnik calls it "structural competence." But the semiotic character of romantic compositions is not exhausted by tonality. Their syntax depends upon something in addition to the tonality, and their semantic reference is altogether different from it. To discover it requires experience and training in music and in an indefinitely wider context. Subotnik calls the capacity that emerges from this training and experience "stylistic competence."

Subotnik's view of the criticism of classical compositions resembles Rosen's view of the nature of criticism of original works; understanding and appreciating their syntax is very like what Rosen calls "analysis." Her view of the criticism of romantic compositions resembles Kerman's view concerning the need for enlarging the notion of analysis; their nontonal syntax and semantic reference are among the features, important to romantic music, that analysis would discern if broadened in the way he suggests. Her view as to the criticism of compositions of both kinds resembles Beardsley's view concerning configurational understanding; understanding and appreciating the syntax of a composition is understanding how its components fit together in a pattern that characterizes the whole. But Subotnik's view that the criticism of romantic compositions is understanding and appreciating their semantical meaning differs from Beardsley's view on that subject. On his view, the semantical meaning of a compostion is constituted by some of its own properties; and its discernment can be no part of criticism. While on her view, the semantical meaning of a romantic composition is something quite different from the composition, and discovering it for oneself and others, an essential element in criticism of it.

In his essay, "Music Criticism: Practice and Malpractice," Karl Aschenbrenner is also concerned with criticism, but especially with criticism of new atonal music. He reminds us that music, in company with the other arts, has changed radically in recent years. New compositions differ markedly from the traditional, and audiences often cannot take them in. Still, they are quite willing to appreciate the new; and Aschenbrenner contends that criticism should assume a more effective role in helping them do so. He develops his position by pointing to a similarity between traditional and new compositions, by considering the source of standards by which all are judged, by describing the task of criticism generally, and by indicating the ways in which it treats the new music properly and improperly—by indicating its practice and malpractice.

All compositions of music, both traditional and new, are made from sounds; and all deploy these sounds in a structure, extending through a stretch of time. In traditional music, the sounds are pitches, related by intervals determined by scales; and in the same music, the structure grows out of the intervals that relate the pitches —out of the reference that each tone makes to others by virtue of its interval relations. The new music abandons, in varying degrees, the techniques and instruments and therefore the sounds that are the elements for traditional music; it rejects, in varying degrees, the scalar ordering of pitches that make for intervals and the structure that grows from them, favoring instead the twelve-tone scale and serial structure, or materials and structures that differ even more radically from those of tonality. Still, its compositions, like those of traditional music, are sounds in a temporal structure, however much the sounds differ from the traditional, and the structure from that based upon the system of tonality.

An audience, bewildered by a new composition, but willing to appreciate it, may look for help to its composer. His intimate acquaintance with his composition might enable him to bring out features that the audience had missed, and that give the composition intelligibility and value. The difficulty is that since the composition is his own creation, he may be inclined to find values in it that no one else can find. But if the audience looks to the critic, it may well be given a judgment based upon a comparison of the composition with a standard derived from the class to which the critic takes the composition to belong—a comparison with a historical universal. This judgment will overlook the individuality of the composition, which is, nonetheless, what the bewildered audience is seeking.

Searching for the source of standards for judging a composition, we come quickly to what seems to be a paradox. The standard cannot be found in the opinions of the composer; for even though he knows the composition in all its individuality better than any other person does, he is too partial to be trusted. Nor can it be found in the opinions of the critic; he applies to the composition a standard that is not relevant. Aschenbrenner dispels the appearance of paradox by observing that the standard for evaluating any composition is found in no one's opinions concerning it, but in that composition itself—in the capacity of its sounds or structure to evoke feelings of favor or disfavor in the listener.

The critic's task is to awaken feelings in the audience that are appropriate to the composition criticized. He accomplishes this task by pronouncing his judgment of value, and, more important, by characterizing the sounds or structure in such a way as to support his evaluation. Each "characterization" (Aschenbrenner's term) contains two components. The "conceptual component" attributes certain features to the composition. The "appraisive component" betokens the critic's feeling toward it, awakened by those features. It is these feelings (or rather the capacity to awaken them) that give value to the composition. The critic's characterizations support his value judgment by describing objective features of the composition, and by expressing feelings they awaken.

The critic (Aschenbrenner says the "ideal critic") brings to music an extensive vocabulary of characterizing terms; their conceptual components enable him to discriminate in the music a greater variety of objective features than can the untutored listener. Their appraisive components release a corresponding variety of feelings toward the composition by virtue of its objective features. And as Aschenbrenner remarks, "the proper hearing of music is inherently critical."[8] It is to this critical hearing that the bewildered, but willing, audience aspires; and it is in order to bring that audience to such a hearing, i.e., to bring it to agree with him in his own hearing of it, that the critic characterizes and thereby judges the composition.

This agreement is, in part, an agreement of description. If the composition shows the inversion of a subject, the critic will endeavor to enable the audience to hear the truth of that description. But while the critic must aim at this agreement, his more important end is agreement in feeling toward the composition that follows on agreement of description. The critic's task is to advance the audience's agreement with his own critical hearing by adroit characterization—to enable it to find in the composition the value that his critical vocabulary and sensitivity make evident to himself.

The practice of criticism is well conducted provided that the critic keeps his mind open to all objective features of the composition, and responds in an unbiased way with feelings that are strong and readily varied. But music criticism in our day suffers from four forms of malpractice. First, it sometimes refuses to characterize its subjects, substituting description of them for appraisal. This malpractice gives no guidance to the audience's emotional response. Secondly, it sometimes refuses to give the negative characterizations it honestly feels, and, consequently, the negative judgments toward which it is genuinely inclined. Wanting to encourage the new music, it does not speak its mind. Again, the audience receives no guidance. Thirdly, the bias of the critic sometimes makes him unable to make use of all the resources of criticism. Favoring works that are unified and disfavoring those that are chaotic, he is likely not to notice that a work is varied or monotonous. Still, these neglected traits may be capable of evoking feeling, and not to characterize a work as possessing them is to fail to guide the audience to a full appreciation of the composition criticized. Fourthly, criticism sometimes fails to treat the new music as music. Traditional music, formed within the system of tonality, presents a sound and structure relatively accessible to critic and to audience. But the new music, formed in systems more remote from the usual mode of musical perception, presents a sound that is unfamiliar and a structure almost amorphous to the ordinary ear. The critic should characterize them both in positive ways when he can, helping the audience toward critical hearing. But he often fails to characterize the sound and structure as what they are preeminently, namely, boring. This fourth malpractice is the most important.

The criticism of music is what the critic does in his effort to enhance the understanding and appreciation of compositions, and each of the authors in this volume describes this effort from a certain perspective. From Rosen's perspective, the effort consists often in showing the influence of earlier compositions upon the composition criticized; but where this genetic understanding cannot be advanced, where an inspired and original composition is his subject, the critic must try, instead, for configurational understanding or analysis. From Kerman's perspective, also, the critic must try for analysis; but this configurational understanding must not be limited to the discernment of pitches, motives, rhythms, and textures in organic relations, but must be extended to the discernment of a configuration of all important elements within the composition and of the entire composition with an undetermined number of other terms in its historical context. From Beardsley's perspective, the critic should describe the composition in such a way as to enable discernment and appreciation of its human qualities; and while it may be understood semantically (it is a sign whose reference is these qualities), the semantic understanding of a composition can play no part in criticism of it. From Subotnik's perspective, criticism must discern the semiotic character of music. In classical compositions, it seeks their tonal syntax or structure, whereas in romantic compositions, it seeks their style—the syntax or tonal structure of their sequences, the nontonal syntax that relates these sequences, and the semantic reference of entire compositions. From Aschenbrenner's perspective, criticism must try to discern the temporal structure—tonal, serial, or what not—in which the elements or the sounds of the composition have been placed, and to assure that the listener enjoys the same feeling toward the composition as does the critic. To this end, the critic must characterize the composition with predicates that express the subjective feelings awakened in him by the objective features descried. Criticism, thus, eventuates in subjective judgments; but properly practiced, it yields subjective judgments that are warranted by an informed, discriminating, and tolerant consideration of the composition judged.

Notes

1. Donald J. Grout, *A History of Western Music* (New York: W. W. Norton and Co., 1960), p. 5.
2. Plato, *Republic*, 475. *The Dialogues of Plato*, ed. B. Jowett (New York: Random House, 1937), 1: 738-39.
3. Aristotle, *Politics* 8.6.1341^{a}10. Cited by Grout, *History of Western Music*, p. 6.
4. Monroe C. Beardsley, "Understanding Music," Chapter 4 in this volume.
5. Joseph Kerman, "The State of Academic Music Criticism," Chapter 3 in this volume.
6. Beardsley, "Understanding Music."
7. Ibid.
8. Karl Aschenbrenner, "Music Criticism: Practice and Malpractice," Chapter 6 in this volume.

2

Influence:
Plagiarism and Inspiration
CHARLES ROSEN

For practice I have also set to music the aria "Non so d'onde viene," which has been so beautifully composed by Bach. Just because I know Bach's setting so well and like it so much, and because it is always ringing in my ears, I wished to try and see whether in spite of all this I could not write an aria totally unlike his. And, indeed, mine does not resemble his in the very least.—Mozart to his father, 28 February 1778

OF ALL CLASSICAL INFLUENCES on Renaissance and baroque literature, the most puzzling to assess is the influence of Plato on La Fontaine; it will serve admirably as a model for what I have to say about music. We know from La Fontaine himself that he loved the writings of Plato. After La Fontaine's death, the Abbé d'Olivet wrote that he had seen the poet's copy of Plato's works (in a Latin translation): "They were annotated in his own hand on every page, and I remarked that most of these notes were maxims of ethics or politics which he planted in his fables."[1] This copy of Plato has not come down to us.

The works of La Fontaine have been studied for allusions to Plato. There are almost none. Scholars have looked for quotations from Plato, with an almost total lack of success. But nobody ever claimed there were any. Reading Plato inspired La Fontaine not to quotation but to original thought. What this original thought was can only be a matter for surmise: in the absence of any documentary evidence, no

An abridged version of this essay first appeared in *Nineteenth Century Music* 4, no. 2 (Fall 1980). I am grateful to Daniel Heartz for drawing my attention to the Mozart letter (Anderson 292) cited in the epigraph, and to Walter Frisch for the information in note 5.

proof of any of our conjectures is possible. The rules of evidence that enable us, on circumstantial grounds, to convict a writer of having been influenced are of no use to us in this case—and it is precisely this case which is the most interesting kind.

The influence of one artist upon another can take a wide variety of forms, from plagiarism, borrowing, and quotation all the way to imitation and eventually to the profound but almost invisible form we have seen with Plato and La Fontaine. About a half-century ago, literary history used to be envisaged almost entirely as a tracing of such influences, and this has not yet completely fallen out of fashion. In the history of the visual arts, it is perhaps the major form of professional activity. Certain periods provide more fertile grounds than others: above all, nineteenth-century writers, artists, and composers seem to have cultivated a knack for being influenced by their predecessors. The unacknowledged, or hidden, Shakespearean quotation is as much a trick of Hazlitt's and of Byron's styles as the hidden borrowing from Renaissance sources is a part of Manet's. Buried romantic allusions to Shakespeare are essentially different from the often tacit references to classical poets like Horace in the works of Pope and his contemporaries. Pope modernized his sources, and his hidden references ennobled their modern context for the connoisseur. The romantic allusions archaize and alienate: they give an exotic flavor to the familiar every-day. Manet's uses of Raphael and Titian are still today a little shocking, while Dürer's adaptations of classical Greek sculpture are dignified and uplifting.

In discussing influence in music, it would be wise to refuse in advance to consider the work of adolescent composers. With the startling exception of Mendelssohn, a very young composer has no style of his own, and he is forced to get one somewhere else. His models have largely a biographical, but not much critical, significance—he may, indeed, reject his early models by the time he reaches his majority.

Plagiarism has an interest for ethics and law, but little for criticism. Even in the case of the most notorious thefts—those of Handel and Coleridge, to take two examples—the outright appropriations are less significant than those in which the borrowed material has been transformed. Nevertheless, it is the process of transformation that raises all the difficulties for study. With plagiarism, we have two works in which some part of both is identical, a part too large for the identity to be fortuitous. This identity establishes beyond a doubt the relationship between the two works. As we move away from such simple situations, that is, as the later artist transforms the borrowed material into something more his own, this relationship is put into question. The critic must still claim an identity between something in the earlier work and the material of the new work. But what gives him the right to maintain this identity except a resemblance which diminishes as the transformation is more thorough? Sometimes·a document is forthcoming in which the later artist acknowledges the source of his inspiration—and, even then, the interpretation of such an admission can rarely be straightforward. When the transformation is an almost total one, evidence for the identity is erased in a work which now appears completely original. The source is likely to seem irrelevant to the critic, because it is not clear by what method he can reach it, although in this case the source is in fact more relevant for criticism than in any other. The most important form of influence is that which provokes the most original and most personal work. If we had La Fontaine's annotations to his copy of Plato, it is by no means certain that we would understand at once what the poet saw in the philosopher.

The range of the problem may be shown first by two examples from Mozart. On 17 May 1789, Mozart wrote a fugal Gigue for Piano (K. 574), in Leipzig, the city of Sebastian Bach and gave it as a present to the court organist. It has a characteristic opening (see example 1A). Haydn's Quartet in C Major op. 20 no. 2 has a fugal gigue as a finale, and it opens as follows (example 1B). The resemblance is obvious (in the descent G-F#-F#-E as part of the basic structure of the tune) and trivial. Such thematic resemblances are a dime-a-dozen. We are aware, of course, that Mozart knew Haydn's op. 20 quartets very well indeed, since he imitated them closely many years before when he began to write string quartets at the age of sixteen.

EXAMPLE 1

EXAMPLE 2

From the second part of Mozart's gigue, however, there is a striking, even astonishing rhythmic change of accent (see example 2A). If the phrasing is correctly played (which is not often the case), the $\frac{6}{8}$ rhythm is suddenly contradicted by a $\frac{2}{4}$—or, more precisely, cut by a $\frac{4}{8}$ grouping enforced by the parallelisms of two staccato and two legato notes (see example 3). More suprisingly, perhaps, there is a

[18]

similar effect in Haydn's gigue (example 2B). Haydn's grouping is more complex and a little less disconcerting: it contrasts (by two staccato, two legato, two staccato eighth-notes) a $\frac{3}{4}$ with the $\frac{6}{8}$ grouping of three and three. It is nonetheless startling; and once heard, it is hard to forget. Mozart evidently remembered and improved on it. Alfred Einstein writes in the third edition of Köchel: "Mozart hat mit diesem Stammbuchblatt dem Genius loci—Bach—gehuldigt, ohne eine Stilkopie zu liefern." If only Mozart had written his gigue in Esterhaz instead of in Leipzig, it would be considered a homage to Haydn.

EXAMPLE 3

The connection between Haydn's Symphony no. 81 in G Major and Mozart's *Prague* Symphony in D Major (K. 504) is more tenuous but more suggestive. Haydn's symphony was written in 1783-84, at just the moment that the friendship between Haydn and Mozart began,[2] the *Prague* was written two or three years later. Example 4 shows the beginning of the two allegros. The contrast between Haydn's

EXAMPLE 4

EXAMPLE 5

BRAHMS

RONDO.
Allegro non troppo.

Second phrase: monophonic obbligato

EXAMPLE 5 *continued*

BEETHOVEN

Second phrase: monophonic obbligato

Third phrase

EXAMPLE 5 *continued*

BRAHMS

Third phrase: descending motif repeated

[poco sostenuto] Cadenza

EXAMPLE 5   *continued*

BEETHOVEN

Descending motif repeated

muscular opening and Mozart's restrained syncopations following the massive introduction could not be more absolute. Yet both have important and unusual things in
common: a soft ostinato on the tonic note that continues for several measures and
the striking introduction on the flat seventh in the third measure. Significant, too, is
the gradual deployment of new motifs as the period continues, including a completely
new rhythmic texture and motif, and a cadence in the last two measures, just before
the theme starts up again.

Was Mozart impressed by Haydn's quiet playing of the flat seventh against a
repeated tonic in the third measure of his allegro, and did he think he could make
even grander use of the device? No proof will ever be forthcoming one way or the
other, nor would it be particularly interesting if it were. We should remark, however,
that the *Prague* is unusual among Mozart's works in employing a particularly
Haydnesque structural effect: the return of the opening theme at the dominant to
establish that key in the exposition. This is only too common in Haydn but rare in
Mozart, although we may find it in the Piano Trio in B-flat Major (K. 502), written a
month before the *Prague* Symphony.

There are other contacts with Haydn's technique to be found in the *Prague*,
particularly in the use of ritornello effects in transitional passages and in the way the
motifs are developed. A study will reveal greater differences, above all in the breadth
of the conception. These differences do not demonstrate any distance from Haydn—it
may have been that Haydn's example stimulated Mozart to something completely
his own, that Haydn provided the most profound form of inspiration. The influence
of Haydn's music on the adolescent Mozart is easy to trace; the influence on the later
Mozart is largely untraceable but may have been just as important. If there was any,
we cannot reconstruct the steps of Mozart's transformation, only guess at them. The
solidity of the study of sources begins to dissolve as the subject becomes more
significant.

Influence of a different nature appears in the nineteenth century, with the choice
of a particular work as a structural model. An example is the finale of Brahms's Piano
Concerto no. 1 in D Minor. The dependence of this movement on the last movement
of Beethoven's Piano Concerto no. 3 in C Minor was remarked by Tovey, but it has
never, as far as I know, been spelled out.[3] The closeness of that dependence, taken
together with the fact that the two pieces sound so different that even the most
cultivated listener is unlikely to be reminded of one by the other, makes this an
interesting case.

The two finales may be described and analyzed to a great extent as if they were the
same piece (see example 5):

Rondo form. Minor key. $\frac{2}{4}$ *Allegro* (Beethoven); *Allegro non troppo* (Brahms). 1st
phrase, 8 measures. Solo piano alone. Opening theme.
2nd phrase. 8 measures. Orchestra repeats the first phrase with pizzicato accompaniment. Solo plays obbligato counterpoint in octaves.
3rd phrase. Second phrase of theme started by solo alone, orchestra entering in the
middle of the phrase. The theme develops a sharp descending motif repeated several
times getting softer (*calando, più dolce*) and slower (*ritard., più sostenuto*).
Cadenza (measured in Brahms). Arpeggiated figuration descending and then as-

cending, ending with a scale that leads directly into the return of the opening phrase, now played by the piano accompanied by the orchestra. Beethoven's scale ascends and Brahms's descends, but that is not an impressive transformation.

After the second theme in the mediant major, the return of the first theme is heralded by extensive arpeggios on the dominant. The opening phrase reappears in the solo, accompanied now by the strings pizzicato.

The middle section of the rondo is a new lyrical theme in the submediant major (A-flat in Beethoven, B-flat in Brahms), appearing first in the orchestra and then accompanied in the solo piano. A staccato fugue (*pp*, Beethoven, *sempre p*, Brahms) follows as a development (m. 230 in Beethoven, m. 238 in Brahms), beginning in the strings, the winds entering later (example 6). Then the first appearance of the main

EXAMPLE 6

theme in the major mode is formed with a drone bass in pastoral style (example 7). (In the Brahms, it is the mediant major, in the Beethoven, more astonishingly, the flat mediant major.) This leads to extensive arpeggios on a dominant pedal followed by brilliant passagework which prepares the return of the opening theme. After the recapitulation, there is a cadenza and a coda in major (in Brahms, a long cadenza and an extensive series of codas).

EXAMPLE 7

This procedure of modeling upon a previous structure is clearly explicit, and equally clearly not intended to be audible to the general public, however much it may add to the appreciation of the connoisseurs. It is akin to the dependence of the finale of Schubert's Piano Sonata in A Major (D. 959) on the finale of Beethoven's Piano Sonata in G Major, op. 31 no. 1 (a relationship demonstrated some years ago independently by Professor Edward T. Cone and myself).[4] The technique has an obvious and superficial resemblance to late medieval parody technique, which we can safely neglect here, but we need to distinguish it carefully from the nineteenth-century composer's use of *quotation*, the thematic allusion to a previous work.

Brahms was a master of allusion, and he generally intended his references to be heard ("Any ass can see that," he is supposed to have said, when one of them was recognized). Opus 1 (the Piano Sonata in C Major) begins with a clear reference to Beethoven's *Hammerklavier:* that, in fact, is why it is opus 1—Brahms's career starts from this quotation (the work is by no means Brahms's first piano sonata). The Scherzo op. 4, begins with a similar quotation. The reference is to Chopin's Scherzo in B-flat Minor (example 8).

EXAMPLE 8

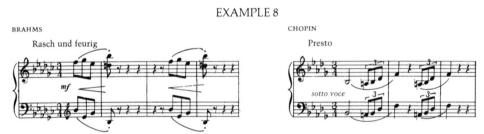

The homage to Chopin does not stop there. A page later in Brahms's scherzo we find a passage that is freely developed from another scherzo of Chopin's, this one in C-sharp minor (example 9). With this, however, we have left behind the device of

EXAMPLE 9

quotation, and we reach a new adaptation. Still later in the Brahms Scherzo op. 4, in the second of the two trios, there is a return to Chopin's B-flat Minor Scherzo with the following lovely passage (example 10).

EXAMPLE 10

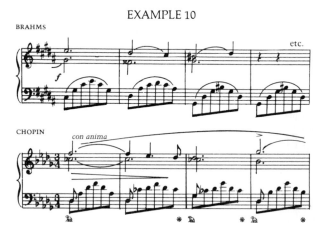

Is this quotation or adaptation? It is derived fairly directly from Chopin. It should be clear why Brahms started his scherzo with an unmistakable allusion to Chopin: having steeped himself in Chopin's style in order to absorb a now canonic conception of the virtuoso piano scherzo, Brahms displays the thematic reference at the opening in order to signal the presence of imitation. The listener who is also a connoisseur is notified in advance that his appreciation of the work about to be played will be enhanced if he recognizes the imitation and savors the finesse with which it has been carried out.[5] With Brahms, we reach a composer whose music we cannot fully appreciate—at a certain level, at any rate—without becoming aware of the influences which went into its making, in exactly the same way that it is difficult to make sense of Mendelssohn's *Reformation* Symphony without recognizing the chorale tunes. Influence for Brahms was not merely a part of the compositional process, a necessary fact of creative life: he incorporated it as part of the symbolic structure of the work, its iconography. We might even conjecture that the overt references are often there as signals, to call attention to others less obvious, almost undetectable.

The two open references to Beethoven's *Emperor* Concerto made by Brahms's Piano Concerto no. 2 in B-flat Major are placed in such crucial places, so set in relief, in fact, that they must be understood as staking a claim. This work, we are informed by these open references, is intended to follow upon the tradition left off by Beethoven. Opening the first movement with a cadenza for the soloist points directly to the *Emperor:* Brahms has altered the scheme only to make room for an initial statement of the main theme by the orchestra (with additional antiphonal effects from the piano that derive from Mozart's Concerto in E-flat, K. 271). Enlarging the form set by the *Emperor* to include a brief initial statement of the theme was an obvious step—so clearly the next thing to do that Beethoven himself tried this out in an elaborate sketch for a sixth piano concerto that was probably unknown to Brahms.[6]

The second reference is a thematic, as well as a structural, quotation. Compare the entrance of the soloist in the slow movements of the *Emperor* and the Brahms concertos (example 11). Brahms adds two introductory measures, and then produces an ornamented version of Beethoven's music, a magnificent homage. This sort of allusion is like the modernized quotation from Horace practiced by poets of the time

BEETHOVEN

EXAMPLE 11

BRAHMS

of Pope. It creates an intimate link between poet and educated reader, composer and professional musician—and excludes the ordinary reader and listener. It also acknowledges the existence of a previous classical style, an aspiration to recreate it, and an affirmation that such a recreation is no longer possible on naive or independent terms. The control of style is now not merely willed but self-conscious.

These overt allusions warn us of the presence of more recondite imitations. Perhaps the most interesting of the latter is the use Brahms makes of a striking passage in the coda of the first movement of the *Emperor* for the identical place in his own first movement (see example 12). What characterizes this passage is the *pianissimo* chromatic descent followed by the first phrase of the main theme *fortissimo*, the reduction of this to a few notes, the arrangement of this fragment in a rising sequence, and the striking irregularity of the sequence in its antiphonal division between piano and orchestra. All of these qualities are faithfully reproduced by Brahms (example 13). In keeping with his dislike of pure orchestral effect, Brahms has slightly attenuated the antiphonal nature of the conception, although it is still clearly in evidence in his

EXAMPLE 12

BEETHOVEN

EXAMPLE 13

EXAMPLE 13 *continued*

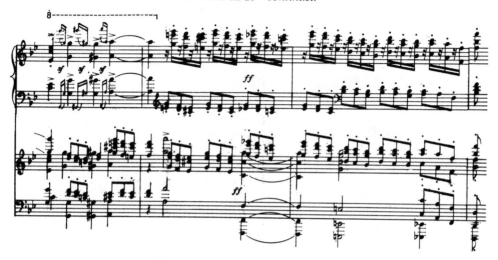

version: in place of solo against orchestra, it has become solo and strings against winds.

For the scherzo of the concerto, Brahms has no model available from the Beethoven piano concertos (although he is able to incorporate reminiscences of the Ninth Symphony). The basic model is, once again, Chopin. We have seen that Brahms's knowledge of Chopin's scherzos was profound: here he uses the E-Major Scherzo no. 4. Both works are built on a rigid, underlying, four-measure structure in which the basic grouping of measures remains unaltered, while the phrases appear supple because they start on the second measure of a group. This imposes a long beat over the fast tempo as one hears each four-measure unit almost as one long measure, but the melodies take irregular forms within this. Brahms's second theme is particularly striking. It appears to be an eleven-measure theme, but it clearly starts in the second measure of a unit (see example 14). (I have annotated the passage in order to show the outer regularity of the inner irregularity.) The technique is derived directly from Chopin (see example 15). In both movements, the four-measure grouping is overridden, largely by avoiding a coincidence between the first measure of a unit and the opening of a phrase.

The first page of Brahms's finale parades a curious combination of references. The basic model for the first theme is still the scheme formulated by Beethoven in the Third Piano Concerto and already used by Brahms. To recapitulate the plan:

1. First phrase: main theme in solo part,
2. First phrase repeated by orchestra, with monophonic obbligato in solo,
3. Second phrase in solo, accompanied, repeating motif dying away,
4. Cadenza with scale leading back to,
5. First phrase.

So much is faithfully reproduced by Brahms, except that the cadenza is reduced to its final scale alone with an added trill (example 16).

EXAMPLE 14

BRAHMS

The opening phrase, however, is based on another Beethoven model, the opening of the finale of the Fourth Piano Concerto in G Major (example 17). Beethoven's phrase is extraordinary for its opening on the subdominant, reaching the tonic only towards the end of its second half. This very striking concept is plain in Brahms, and

EXAMPLE 15

CHOPIN

EXAMPLE 16

BRAHMS

EXAMPLE 16 *continued*

BRAHMS

EXAMPLE 16 *continued*

BRAHMS

EXAMPLE 17

BEETHOVEN

he is obviously anxious for the connoisseur to recognize the source, as he imitates the orchestration of an accompaniment by a single string line. The substitution of the viola for the solo cello proclaims Brahms's creative independence.

This is not the only time that Brahms used a scheme to be found in Beethoven's G-Major Concerto. The most astonishing feature of the opening movement of that work is its first measures. The obvious cause for surprise is the instrumentation, a quiet opening in the solo, followed by the orchestra. For the connoisseur, however, the most significant feature is the remote harmony with which the second phrase opens. It gives a wonderful sense of breadth and of space.

Brahms's allusion is for connoisseurs alone, and may be found in the first sixteen measures of the Violin Concerto. For a contrast of solo and orchestra, Brahms substitutes a contrast of texture and spacing: he always disliked showy orchestral effects, and his practice of bringing in unusual instruments like the harp or triangle so that their presence at first goes unremarked has often been observed. For Beethoven's V of vi, Brahms substitutes the even more remote triad of the flat seventh degree. Achieved by much the same means, the sense of breadth and space is equally grand, harmonically more striking. (At this stage in his career Brahms's borrowings are generally heightenings: after the cadenza of this concerto, he borrows from Beethoven's Violin Concerto the device of having the main theme return softly, high on the violin's E string, but he sustains it much longer and with greater intensity.)

This last borrowing from the Fourth Piano Concerto may be doubted, and I have proposed it deliberately because it is dubious (although I cannot believe that such a parallelism could have occurred to me and not to Brahms, who knew the music of Beethoven better than any other musician in history). It approaches the sort of transformation of a model which is so complete that it is almost undetectable and certainly unprovable without a signed affidavit from the composer admitting the borrowing. This is hardly likely to turn up. What Brahms had to say about his relation to history and to the past, he let his music say for him. This goes to show that when the study of sources is at its most interesting, it becomes indistinguishable from pure musical analysis.

Notes

1. Quoted in La Fontaine, *Oevres diverses*, ed. Pierre Clarac, Bibliothèque de la Pléiade (Paris: Gallimard, 1942), 2: 984.

2. The most likely starting point is 1784. See H. C. Robbins Landon, *Haydn: Chronicle and Works*, vol. 2 (Bloomington: Indiana University Press, 1978), p. 509.

3. Donald F. Tovey, *Essays in Musical Analysis*, vol. 3, *Concertos* (London: Oxford University Press, 1936), pp. 74, 118.

4. See Edward T. Cone, "Schubert's Beethoven," *Musical Quarterly* 56 (1970): 779-93, and Charles Rosen, *The Classical Style* (New York, 1971), pp. 456-58.

5. In light of the obvious indebtedness to Chopin, it is surprising that Brahms claimed to have known no Chopin when writing the E-flat-Minor Scherzo. This is the piece that Liszt sightread from manuscript during Brahm's legendary visit to Weimar in 1853. The pianist William Mason, who was present, reports that after the performance Joachim Raff remarked on the resemblance of the opening of the Scherzo to Chopin's B-flat-Minor, but "Brahms said that he had never seen or heard any of Chopin's compositions" (Mason, *Memories of a Musical Life* [New York, 1902], p. 129).

6. See Lewis Lockwood, "Beethoven's Unfinished Piano Concerto of 1815: Sources and Problems," *Musical Quarterly* 56 (1970): 624-46.

3

The State of
Academic Music Criticism

JOSEPH KERMAN

Stanley Cavell's essay "Music Discomposed," in *Must We Mean What We Say?* (1969), has been widely noticed by musicians. Cavell, a philosopher who has written a good deal about aesthetics and about music, literature, and film, remarks that the questions critics ask about works of art, and their answers, if any, need to be accepted as "philosophical data" for the study of aesthetics, alongside the works of art themselves. "Of course," he adds, "not just *any* critic's response can be so taken. And this suggests a further methodological principle in philosophizing about art. It seems obvious enough that in setting out to speak about the arts one begins with a rough canon of the objects to be spoken about. It seems to me equally necessary, in appealing to the criticism of art for philosophical data, that one begin with a rough canon of criticism which is then not repudiated in the philosophy to follow."[1] What I would like to discuss here is the current state of this rough canon of criticism as it applies to the art of music.

First I must make clear my position on a problem of terminology. Cavell ran right into this problem in his essay, which takes as its point of departure the post-Webern serial music of the 1940s, together with the technical writing about it fostered by the influential journals *Die Reihe*, in Germany, and *Perspectives of New Music*, in America. This writing is a branch of the discipline that musicians call "analysis." "If criticism has as its impulse and excuse the opening of access between the artist and his audience, giving voice to the legitimate claims of both, then there is small criticism in these pages,"[2] observed Cavell, and so he was unwilling to treat the musical analysis he was dealing with as criticism. He fell back on the term "philosophy" as a rather unsatisfactory cover for the writing in question.

Other commentators who have dealt with music criticism in recent years, either as a central issue or as a tangential one—Arthur Berger, Edward T. Cone,[3] David Lewin, Leonard B. Meyer, Robert P. Morgan, and Leo Treitler—have shown the same reluctance to affiliate analysis and criticism. Indeed, some words of my own, written about fifteen years ago, can perhaps be taken as representative: "Criticism does not exist yet on the American music-academic scene, but something does exist which may feel rather like it, theory and analysis. . . . Analysis seems too preoccupied with its own inner techniques, too fascinated by its own 'logic,' and too sorely tempted by its own private pedantries, to confront the work of art in its proper aesthetic terms. Theory and analysis are not equivalent to criticism, then, but they are pursuing techniques of vital interest to criticism. They represent a force and a positive one in the academic climate of music."[4]

Fifteen years later, I can only regard this as waffling. According to the *Harvard Dictionary of Music*, the true focus of analysis, once it gets past the taxonomic stage, is on "the synthetic element and the functional significance of the musical detail." Analysis sets out to discern and demonstrate the functional coherence of individual works of art, or, as is often said, their "organic unity," and that is one of the things —one of the main things—that people outside of music mean by criticism. If in a typical musical analysis the work of art is studied in its own self-defined terms, that too is a characteristic strategy of some major strains of twentieth-century criticism. We might like criticism to meet broader criteria, but there it is. Perhaps musical analysis, as an eminently professional process, fails to "open access between the artist and his audience," and perhaps it does indeed fail "to confront the work of art in its proper aesthetic terms"—such failures, too, are not unknown in the criticism of literature or the other arts. Many tasks are ritually urged on criticism that cannot be incorporated into the concept of criticism itself. In other words, I do not see that the criteria suggested above can be included in a definition of criticism which corresponds to the practice of modern critics. We may consider it very desirable that criticism meet these criteria, but we cannot reasonably insist on it. What we have here is a matter for adjustment between music critics of different persuasions, rather than some sort of stand-off between the adherents of distinct disciplines.

It may be objected that musical analysts claim to be working with objective methodologies that leave no place for aesthetic criteria, for the consideration of value. If so, the reluctance of so many writers to subsume analysis under criticism might be understandable. But are these claims true? Are they, indeed, even seriously entered?

Certainly the original masters of analysis left no doubt that for them analysis was an essential adjunct to a fully articulated aesthetic value system. Heinrich Schenker always insisted on the superiority of the towering products of the German musical genius. Sir Donald Tovey pontificated about "the main stream of music" and on occasion developed this metaphor in considerable detail. It is only in more recent times that analysts have avoided value judgments and adapted their work to a format of strictly corrigible propositions, mathematical equations, set-theory formu-lations, and the like—all this, apparently, in an effort to achieve the objective status and hence the authority of scientific inquiry. Articles on music composed after 1950, in particular, as Cavell noted, appear sometimes to mimic scientific papers in the way that South American bugs and flies will mimic the dreaded carpenter wasp. In a somewhat different adaptation, the distinguished analyst Allen Forte once wrote an entire small book, *The Compositional Matrix*, from which all affective or valuational terms (such as "nice" or "good") were meticulously excluded. The same tendency is evident in much of the recent periodical literature.

But it scarcely goes unnoticed that the subject of Forte's monograph is not a symphony by Sammartini or a quartet by Gyrowetz, but a late sonata by Beethoven, the Sonata in E Major op. 109, a work that Forte accepts without question as a masterpiece—without question, and also without discussion. Indeed, this monograph sheds a specially pure light on the archetypal procedure of musical analysis. This branch of criticism takes the masterpiece status of its subject matter as a *donnée* and then proceeds to lavish its whole attention on the demonstration of its inner coherence. Aesthetic judgment is concentrated tacitly on the initial choice of material to be analyzed; then the analysis itself, which may be conducted with the greatest subtlety and rigor, can treat artistic value only casually, or in the extreme case of Forte's monograph, not at all. Another way of putting it is that the question of artistic value is at the same time absolutely basic and begged, begged consistently and programmatically.

In fact, it seems to me that the true intellectual milieu of analysis is not science but ideology. I do not think we can understand analysis and the important role it plays in today's academic music scene on logical, intellectual, or purely technical grounds. We need to understand something of its underlying ideology, and this in turn requires some consideration of its historical context. Robert P. Morgan is an analyst who has reminded us on a number of occasions that his discipline must be viewed as a product of its time: this as a corollary to his conviction that it must also change with the times. The following historical analysis owes something to Morgan's but is, I think, framed more radically, or at any rate, more polemically.

By ideology I mean a fairly coherent set of ideas brought together not for strictly intellectual purposes, but in the service of some strongly held communal belief. Operative here is the orthodox belief, still held over from the late nineteenth century, in the overriding aesthetic value of the instrumental music of the great German tradition. Of this the central monuments are the fugues and some other instrumental compositions of Bach and the sonatas, string quartets, and symphonies of Mozart, Beethoven, and Brahms.

Viennese or pan-German in origin, and certainly profoundly guided by nationalistic passions, this ideology took hold in other countries, depending on the strength or weakness of their native musical traditions. It had its strongest attraction in Britain and America; France embraced it somewhat; Italy not at all. The ideology drew to itself many familiar currents of nineteenth-century thought about art and music. Among these were an essentially mystical idea about spontaneity and authenticity in musical performance, a romantic myth (owing much to the example of Beethoven) that cast the artist as sage and suffering hero, and—most important for the present purpose—a strain of Hegelian aesthetic philosophy that runs from Schopenhauer to Susanne K. Langer with an important backtrack by way of Eduard Hanslick.

For Hanslick, instrumental music was the only "pure" form of the art, and words, librettos, titles, and programs, which seem to link music to the feelings of ordinary, impure life, were to be disregarded or deplored. Music, in Hanslick's famous phrase, is "sounding form in motion." Later aestheticians such as Langer have labored to preserve his central insight without denying, as Hanslick did, that music was anything more than that. The concept is an important one for the essential criterion of value that is built into the ideology. For if music is only "sounding form," the only meaningful study of music is formalistic; and while Hanslick was not an analyst, later critics took it upon themselves to analyze music's "sounding form" in the conviction that this was equivalent to its content. To these analyst-critics, content (however defined) was not a matter of indifference. The music they analyzed was that of the great German tradition.

Their vision was and is of a perfect, organic relation among all the analyzable parts of a musical masterpiece. Increasingly sophisticated techniques of analysis attempt to show how all aspects or "parameters" or "domains" of the masterpiece perform their function for the total structure. Critics who differ vastly from one another in their methods, styles, and emphases still view the work of art ultimately as an organism in this sense. From the standpoint of the ruling ideology, analysis exists for the purpose of demonstrating organicism, and organicism exists for the purpose of validating a certain body of works of art.

I do not, of course, ignore that broader philosophical movement of the late eighteenth and early nineteenth centuries which focused on organicism and which some musicologists have recently been trying to relate to the development of musical style. But together with this historical process went an ideological one, in the service of which the concept of organicism began to lead a charmed existence. Organicism can be seen not only as a historical force that played into the great German tradition but also as the principle that seemed essential to validate that tradition. The ideological resonance of organicism continued long past the time of its historical impetus.

The origins of the ideology can be traced back to the famous biography of Bach published in 1802 by J. N. Forkel, director of music at the University of Göttingen and the first real German musicologist. "Bach united with his great and lofty style the most refined elegance and the greatest precision in the single parts that compose the great whole," wrote Forkel in his exordium to this work. "He thought the whole could not be perfect if anything were wanting to the perfect precision of the single parts. . . . And this man, the greatest musical poet and the greatest musical orator that ever existed, and probably ever will exist, was a German. Let his country be proud of him; let it be proud, but, at the same time, worthy of him!"[5] We can see the concept of the musical organism taking form with the new attention given to fugue in the early nineteenth century. There was a swift Viennese co-option only a few years later, when E.T.A. Hoffmann began to view Haydn, Mozart, and Beethoven with much the same reverence as we do today, and marveled at the way works such as Beethoven's Fifth Symphony seem to grow from a single theme as though from a Goethean *Urpflanz*. The first great ideological crisis was precipitated by Richard Wagner: Wagner, who could not launch a paper boat without making waves, let alone a revolutionary theory of opera. As Wagner asserted his claim to the Beethovenian succession, the youthful Brahms and his imperious friend Joseph Joachim proclaimed their opposition to symphonic poems, music-dramas, and other such novelties. Hanslick had already closed ranks around the concept of purely instrumental music. He soon came to support Brahms, the most instrumentally minded as well as the most traditionally minded of all the great nineteenth-century composers.

The ideology did not receive its full articulation, however, until the music in which it was rooted came under serious attack. This occurred around 1900, when tonality, the seeming linchpin of the entire system, began to slip in Germany as well as elsewhere. Lines of defense were formed at what Virgil Thomson used to call "the Brahms line," first in opposition to Richard Strauss and then to Arnold Schoenberg. The situation was exacerbated after 1920, when Schoenberg, in an astonishing new co-option, presented himself and his music as the true continuation of the Viennese tradition. It is against the background of this new crisis that we must see the work of the founding fathers of analysis.

Schenker was born in 1868, Tovey in 1875. The first significant writings of both men, which appeared shortly after 1900, are peppered with polemics and were obviously conceived as a defense against the new modernism. Tovey was no Viennese, of course—Balliol was his beat, and before that Eton—but over and above the general reliance of Victorian England on German music and musical thought, he himself was deeply influenced by the aging Joachim. Concentration on the sphere of harmony and the larger harmony, namely, tonality, led Tovey ultimately to the organicist position, though he was never as dogmatic in this regard as the Germans. In his major essays on the Schubert String Quintet in C and the Beethoven Quartet in C-sharp Minor, op. 131, he went beyond his usual terminus, the individual movement, and saw tonality inspiring the whole work, with each "key area" conceived of as a functional element in the total structure. And in what he called the "superb rhetoric" of Bach's F-sharp minor setting of "Aus tiefer Noth," in the *Clavier-übung*, Part III—a chorale in which the melodic and rhythmic substance of the given cantus firmus is drawn into all of the polyphonic voice parts according to a rigorous system, so that every note is practically predetermined by an external scheme—Tovey found unshakable evidence that form in art is equivalent to content. "The process miscalled by Horace the concealment of art," wrote Tovey, "is the sublimation of technique into aesthetic results."

In many ways Tovey was a typical product of the *litterae humaniores* at the Oxford of Jowett and Bradley. He came by his neo-Hegelianism honestly. Schenker was equally a typical product of the Vienna Conservatory, where the great systematic theorist Simon Sechter had been the teacher of Bruckner, himself the teacher of Schenker. Slowly, stage by stage throughout his career, Schenker labored to construct a grandiose general theory to account for all the music of the great tradition. Tovey's analytical method may be said to involve a reduction of the melodic surface of music to the level of the articulated system of tonality. Schenker's involved a much more systematic reduction to the level of a single triad, the tonic triad. In his famous series of formalized reductions, he analyzed music on foreground, middle-ground, and background levels—the latter comprising *Urlinie* and *Ursatz*, a drastically simple horizontalization of the vertical sonority of the tonic triad. (We shall see an example of such an *Ursatz* later.) The concept of hierarchies or levels and the technique of their manipulation constituted Schenker's most powerful legacy to the structuralist future.

Beethoven occupied the dead center of Schenker's value system, as well as of Tovey's. Schenker's most exhaustive studies concern Beethoven's third, fifth, and ninth symphonies and the late piano sonatas. Indeed, the list of some fifty compositions that Schenker discussed formally and at full length presents a striking picture of musical orthodoxy. With few exceptions (including, most honorably, those late sonatas), they are drawn from the stable of symphony orchestra warhorses and the piano teachers' rabbit hutch. In this tacit acceptance of received opinion as to the canon of music's masterpieces, Schenker exemplifies one aspect of the discipline of analysis more clearly than any of its other practitioners.

His work looms so large in academic music criticism at the moment that analysis is sometimes equated with "Schenkerism," as it is called. However, the movement is much broader, and therefore more significant, than any intellectual current that was the province of just one man and his disciples could be. Schenker is not the only impressive and influential figure among the older analysts. I have already mentioned Tovey. Rudolph Réti, a follower at one time of Schoenberg and later an emigré to America, developed a nineteenth-century strain of analysis based not on tonality, line, or triad, but on motif. Réti's demonstrations of the hidden identity of all themes in a musical composition—a sort of poor man's organicism—has had a particular impact in Britain. Alfred Lorenz, also originally from Vienna, extended organic analysis over a larger span than had been thought possible—and into forbidden territory, the four great music-dramas of Richard Wagner. While modern Wagner scholars seem not to tire of disproving and rejecting Lorenz's work, it receives sympathetic attention from the Verdians, among others. It is possible that both Réti and Lorenz have been written off a little too hastily by modern American academics.

More important—indeed, crucial—is the role of Schoenberg himself in our story. In his relatively limited body of writings on music, Schoenberg showed himself to be a brilliant theorist and critic, and, justly enough, the fact that he was the composer he was gave those writings immense authority.

Schoenberg's really decisive insight, I think, was to conceive of a way of continuing the great tradition while negating what everyone else felt to be at its very core, namely, tonality. He grasped the fact that what was central to the ideology was not triad and tonality, as Schenker and Tovey believed, but organicism. In his atonal, pre-serial works written just before World War I, Schoenberg worked out a music in which functional relations were established more and more subtly on the motivic, rhythmic, textural, and indeed the pitch level, with less and less reliance on the traditional configurations of tonality. So for Schoenberg, Brahms was the true "progressive" of the late nineteenth century, as he put it in the title of a famous essay—Brahms, who had refined the art of motivic variation, rather than Wagner, who had refined and attenuated tonality to the breaking point. Twelve-tone serialism was not far off, and in retrospect, one can see that the ideal of "total organization," which was to be formulated by the new serialists after World War II, was implicit from the start.

Schoenberg himself was never interested in developing the sort of analysis that has subsequently been practiced on his own and other serial music. But once he had entered his formidable claim for inclusion within the great tradition, it was inevitable that a branch of analysis would spring up to validate that claim. For analysis, as I have already said, exists to articulate the concept of organicism, which in turn exists as the value system of the ideology; and while the validation provided by analysis was not really necessary for the Viennese classics, it became more and more necessary for the music of each succeeding generation. What Schenker did for Beethoven and Lorenz did for Wagner, Milton Babbitt and others did later for Schoenberg, Berg, and Webern.

The universal impetus behind analysis was expressed with particular innocence by Réti when he recalled asking himself as a young student why every note in a Beethoven sonata should be exactly *that* note, rather than some other. Réti dedicated his career as an analyst to finding an objective answer to this question. And questions of the sort can indeed be answered with the totally organized serial music of the 1950s. Every pitch, rhythm, timbre, dynamic, envelope, etc., can be derived by means of simple or slightly less simple mathematics from the work's "precompositional assumptions." Whether this derivation provides the *right* answer—that, to be sure, is another question. But the answer provided by serial analysis is, undeniably, objective.

I come at last, after this lengthy historical digression, to the current state of music criticism in the American academy. Analysis, as I have already indicated, is the main, almost the exclusive, type of criticism practiced in our major music departments. Moreover, I believe that analysis supplies the chief mental spark that can be detected in those departments. They also cultivate musicology, involving mainly historiography and quasi-scientific scholarly research in music; this field is considerably larger than analysis, and better organized. But American musicology in its academic phase—which has now lasted thirty or forty years—seems to me to have produced relatively little of intellectual interest. One is reminded of the state of literary studies in the 1930s; what has been assembled is an impressive mass of facts and figures about music of the past, codified into strictly nonevaluative histories, editions, bibliographies, and the like. Musical analysis has also reminded many observers of the New Criticism, which arose at that time. This analogy, though it is not one that will survive much scrutiny, does point to one of the constants of intellectual life as this applies to the arts: as intellectual stimulus, positivistic history is always at a disadvantage beside criticism. It is precisely because, and only because, analysis is a kind of criticism that it has gained its considerable force and authority on the American academic scene.

Still, as the years and the decades go by, the predominant position of analysis grows more and more paradoxical—paradoxical, because the great German tradition of instrumental music which analysis supports no longer enjoys the unique status it did for the generation of Schenker and Tovey and Schoenberg. There is no need to enlarge on the various factors that have so drastically changed the climate for the consumption and appreciation of music today: the wide variety of music made available by musicological unearthings, on the one hand, and recording technology and marketry on the other; the public's seemingly insatiable hunger for opera of all sorts; the growing involvement with non-Western music, popular music, and quasi-popular music; and also a pervasive general disbelief in hierarchies of value. It is not that we see less, now, in the German masters. But they no longer shut out our perspective on great bodies of other music, new and old.

Another factor, I think, stems from the crisis in which musical composition has for some time found itself. Heretofore the great tradition had been felt to exist in a permanent condition of organic evolution, moving always onward (if not always upward) into the future, into what Wagner confidently called *Die Musik der Zukunft* and what we were still calling "New Music" with the same upbeat accent in the 1950s. Forkel saw the German tradition originating with Bach; E.T.A. Hoffmann saw Beethoven following from Haydn and Mozart; and Schumann, when he turned resolutely from songs and piano pieces to fugues and symphonies, tactfully added his own name. Less tactfully, Wagner did the same. Hanslick countered with Brahms, Adorno nominated Mahler and Schoenberg, and it was still possible in the 1960s to think of Karlheinz Stockhausen, followed at a discreet distance even—who could tell?—by some non-German figures. Now that there are no candidates from the 1970s, a void has been discovered very close to the center of the ideology.

The paradox has been working itself out in recent American analysis. True, a newly published anthology, *Readings in Schenker Analysis*, holds primly to the traditional core of J. S. and C.P.E. Bach, Mozart, Beethoven, Schubert, Schumann, and Brahms. But for more and more analysts it has become a matter of importance—perhaps of supreme importance—to extend the technique to all the music they care deeply about. That is the impetus behind serial analysis, the most impressive American contribution to the discipline at large, which was developed under the general inspiration of Milton Babbitt at Princeton in the late 1940s and 1950s. It is the impetus behind efforts such as that of Morgan and others to extend analysis to the so-called nonteleological music of the 1960s and 1970s. At the other end of the historical spectrum, analyses of pre-Bach, pretonal music were published as early as the 1950s by Felix Salzer, Schenker's most influential follower in this country. Salzer has also sponsored other such analyses in the current periodical *Music Forum*. More or less Lorenzian methods have been applied to the Verdi operas. Other music with words and programs has also been subjected to analytical treatment: the Schumann song cycle *Dichterliebe*, for example, and Berlioz's *Requiem* and *Symphonie fantastique*. The blanket extension of analysis to genres with words and programs has important theoretical implications, of course. For in spite of Hanslick, the verbal messages included with a musical composition have a strong prima facie claim to be counted in with its content, along with its analyzable "sounding form."

These new analyses are, as always, conducted at different levels of sophistication and insight. Even the best of them leave the reader uneasy. They come up with fascinating and undoubtedly relevant data; yet one always has a sinking feeling that something vital has been overlooked. For however heavily we may weight the criterion of organicism in dealing with the masterpieces of German instrumental music, we know that it is less important for other music that we value. This music may really not be "organic" in any useful sense of the word, or its "organicism" may be a more or less automatic and trivial characteristic. Its aesthetic value must depend on other criteria. Cannot a criticism be developed that will explain, validate, or just illuminate these other musical traditions?

The obvious answer would seem to be yes, and one can indeed point to a number of recent efforts along these lines. These efforts have not been followed up to any significant extent, however—at least not yet. Musicians in the academic orbit have always dragged their feet when it comes to developing alternative modes of criticism. This is as true of the musicologists as of the analysts, and of the large, less clearly defined group of musicians whose inclinations may be described as broadly humanistic and who care about musicology and analysis without having made a full commitment to either (for example, the constituency of the College Music Society). Among these many people, it is not uncommon to hear criticism invoked, discussed in general terms, sometimes praised, sometimes even practiced, and occasionally even practiced well. But there seems to be a general disinclination or inability to formalize—much less to institutionalize—the discipline on any scale broader than that of analysis.

There is a real problem here that I do not believe can be attributed entirely to some massive failure of imagination or intellectual nerve. I prefer to believe that at least part of the problem stems from the prestige of analysis, or, to put it more accurately, from the genuine power of analysis which is the source of that prestige. For analysis, taken on its own terms, is one of the most deeply satisfying of all known critical systems. "Music has, among the arts, the most, perhaps the only, systematic and precise vocabulary for the description and analysis of its object,"[6] writes Cavell, more than a little enviously; for he writes as one who knows how much more fully one can fix a melodic line as compared to a line in a drawing, or a musical rhythm as compared to a poetic one, or even an ambiguity of harmony as compared to an ambiguity of metaphor. The discipline of analysis has made a very good thing out of the precise, systematic vocabulary that music possesses. But as Cavell goes on to remark, thinking of the nonexistence of what he calls a "humane criticism" of music, "Somehow that possession must itself be a liability: as though one now undertook to criticize a poem or novel armed with complete control of medieval rhetoric but ignorant of the modes of criticism developed in the past two centuries." The liability must stem from the power of analysis and its consequent seductiveness. Its methods are so straightforward, its results so automatic, and its conclusions so easily tested and communicated that every important American critic at the present time has involved or implicated himself centrally with analysis.

This includes critics who would not consider themselves primarily analysts and who would probably be begrudged that epithet by the analysts themselves.[7] Charles Rosen, for example, prefaces *The Classical Style* with a critique of analytical systems en masse; the limitations of Schenker, Tovey, Réti, and others are cataloged incisively. Nevertheless, Rosen's procedure in the book is basically analytical, if by analysis we mean the technical demonstration of the coherence of individual pieces of music. He also presents a trenchant, controversial historical interpretation and a steady stream of brilliant *aperçus* on all aspects of music. But at heart his book is a wonderfully readable and original essay in musical analysis. Rosen speaks not of "organicism," but of "balance" and "coherence," and it is his sensitivity to the harmonic and melodic determinants of these criteria that gives *The Classical Style* its greatest power.

Leonard B. Meyer, in his impressive first book, *Emotion and Meaning in Music*, proposed a comprehensive theory of musical aesthetics. A widely ranging scholar, he moves on in his fourth book, *Explaining Music*, to spell out his recipe for criticism. Again, there are telling arguments against Réti and Schenker, and again the proof of the pudding turns out to be analysis—a detailed exemplary study of the first twenty-one bars of a Beethoven sonata according to the author's own analytical principles. (An even more detailed analysis of another German masterpiece has since appeared in *Critical Inquiry*.)[8] Meyer sees musical events as embodying multiple implications for other events that will ensue, implications that are or are not realized in various ways. This follows perfectly the model of an overriding system of relationships between all musical elements which has always animated analytical thinking.

Finally, there is a recent book called *Beyond Schenkerism*, by a new young writer, Eugene Narmour. This is probably the sharpest, most comprehensive attack on Schenker that has ever appeared; and it culminates in the modest proposal of a new analytical system developed by the attacker. The musician's instinctive tendency is always to choose among rival analytical systems or principles, rather than look for broader alternatives to analysis itself. Where we should be looking is not only Beyond Schenkerism but also Beyond Narmourism.[9]

I dislike seeming to preach in the abstract, especially when I seem to be preaching against, so I shall now sketch out some conceivable alternatives to analysis in reference to the criticism of one particular short piece of music. I have chosen a familiar, standard German-masterpiece-type example, hoping to show how much can and should be done even in the area where analytical methods traditionally work best.

The piece, "Aus meiner Thränen fliessen" (example 1), is the second song in Robert Schumann's song cycle *Dichterliebe*. The poem is from Heine's "Lyrisches Intermezzo" in the *Buch der Lieder*. I have chosen it partly because, in the somewhat overheated words of the analyst Arthur Komar, "in recent years, the song has aroused an extraordinary amount of interest, much of which can be attributed to its selection as the principal illustration of Schenker's analytic technique in Allen Forte's important introductory article on Schenker's theories."[10] In my view, Schenker's analysis of this song, which bids fair to attain exemplary status, shows up the limitations of the discipline as a whole with exemplary clarity. It constitutes a strong argument for alternatives.

Those unacquainted with the Schenker system will be interested in seeing his analysis of the song (example 2).[11] What he called the *foreground sketch* is shown on the bottom line. More than 75 percent of the notes in the actual song have already been reduced away from this; only those considered structurally most important

EXAMPLE 1

remain, with their relative structural weight indicated by the presence or absence of stems, by the note values—half-note forms are more important than quarter-note forms, and so on—and by the beams connecting certain groups of quarter- and half-notes (in this sketch). Above it, the *middleground sketch* carries the reduction one step further, and above that the *background sketch* completes the process. The basic structure of the song is indicated by the unit at the top right of this *Ursatz*: a simple three-step arpeggiation of the A-major triad, going from the third degree, the note C-sharp, to the tonic A by way of B as a passing note in the middle. The unit at the left shows the original thrust toward this same *Urlinie* interrupted at the midpoint; the motion is then resumed and completed as shown at the right. Every middleground

EXAMPLE 2

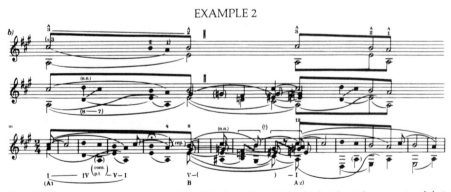

Note: The bass carries an arpeggiation of the fifth down through the third without, however, invalidating the interruption.

and foreground detail can be seen to play its organic role as subsumed by the *Ursatz*. Indeed, the *Ursatz* is indicative of organicism on an ever higher level, for the *Ursätze* of all musical compositions in the great tradition are essentially the same. Although naturally the interruptions differ, and sometimes the tonic triad is arpeggiated $\hat{5}$-$\hat{3}$-$\hat{1}$ or $\hat{8}$-$\hat{5}$-$\hat{3}$-$\hat{1}$, rather than $\hat{3}$-$\hat{1}$, as here, in principle the *Urlinie* always consists of a simple downward arpeggiation of the triad, which Schenker took to be the "chord of nature."

It seems interesting, incidentally, and possibly significant, that this apparently simple song still leaves room for debate as to the precise location of the principal structural tones. Schenker put $\hat{3}$ on the upbeat to bar 1, $\hat{2}$ on the upbeat to bar 9, $\hat{3}$ on the upbeat to bar 13, $\hat{2}$ and $\hat{1}$ in bar 15. Forte proposed a modification: the second $\hat{3}$ on the C-sharp in bar 14 (beat 2). Komar accepts this and proposes another modification: the first $\hat{3}$ on the C-sharp in bar 2. More serious interest might attach to this debate if someone would undertake to show how its outcome affects the way people actually hear, experience, or respond to the music. In the absence of such a demonstration, the whole exercise can seem pretty ridiculous.

As is not infrequently the case with Schenkerian analyses, the fragile artistic content of this song depends quite obviously on features that are skimmed over in the analytical treatment. The song's most striking feature—practically its *raison d'être*, one would think—is the series of paired cadences in the voice and then the piano at the conclusion of lines 2, 4, and 8 of the poem. How are these rather haunting, contradictory stops to be understood (or "heard," as musicians like to say) at the two points within the body of the song? And how are they to be heard at the end? From Schenker's foreground sketch one gathers that in bars 4 and 8 he counted the voice's half cadences as primary, whereas in bar 17 he counted the piano's full cadence. But there is no explanation for this disappointingly conventional interpretation, nor any appreciation of the whole extremely original and suggestive situation, nor indeed any relic of it on the middle- and background levels. The *Ursatz* confuses the issue, for in bars 4 and 8 the cadences lack status because they are regarded simply as details of prolongation, along with many others, and in bars 16-17 they are trivialized because true closure is conceived as happening a bar earlier.

Forte and Komar, with their *Ursatz* revisions, do nothing to help the situation. Ambiguities such as those set up by Schumann's cadences are likely to strike a critic as a good place to focus his investigation. The analyst's instinct is to reduce them out of existence.

Another prime feature of the song burked by Schenker is the climax at the words "Und vor deinem Fenster soll klingen," in line 7. Schumann achieved this by a classical confluence of thickened piano texture, intensified rhythms, a crescendo, and harmonic enrichment by means of chromaticism; for a moment the emotional temperature shoots up into or nearly into the danger zone. Schenker's foreground sketch, so far from "explaining" the chromaticism here, barely acknowledges its existence. Once again, his very first reduction employs too coarse a sieve to catch something of prime importance. Schenker seems often to have derived a sort of grim pleasure from pretending not even to notice certain blatant foreground details in the music he was analyzing.

In this case, the pretense was too much for Forte, who draws attention to what he rightly calls a "striking" chromatic line, an inner line, and to its parallelism to others in the song. The emotional temperature, however, does not interest him, any more than does the symbolism (of which more later); all that concerns him is the fact that the line serves as "an additional means of unification." Forte finds a particularly vexing problem in the G-natural of bars 12-13. Komar too dwells on this as the "major analytic issue" of the whole song.

Neither of these analysts bothers to say (though they surely must see) that both the chromatic G-natural and also the chromatic F-natural in bar 14 give the word *klingen* a richer emotional coloration than either *spriessen* or *werden* found in parallel places earlier in the song. Sooner or later we shall have to retrace the course taken by the composer himself and peek at the words of the poem.

> Aus meinen Thränen spriessen
> Viel blühende Blumen hervor,
> Und meine Seufzer werden
> Ein Nachtigallenchor.
>
> Und wenn du mich lieb hast, Kindchen,
> Schenk' ich dir die Blumen all',
> Und vor dienem Fenster soll klingen
> Das Lied der Nachtigall.

Klingen is a verb applied by the man in the street to coins, wine glasses, and cymbals; poets apply it to the song of nightingales. Was Schumann trying to insist on the poetic credentials of this verb? He certainly declaimed it strangely; the vowel should be short, as of course he knew perfectly well. Also harmonized very richly is the parallel word in the previous couplet—the assonant and no doubt hugely significant word *Kindchen*. So presumably the curious accents in lines 2 and 4 on the words *spriessen* and *werden* (rather than on *Thränen* and *Seufzer*) were planned with *Kindchen* and *klingen* in mind. Schumann's personal reading of the poem begins to take shape. That reading may fairly be suspected of having influenced his musical decisions.

A good deal more can be done along these lines. Musico-poetic analysis is not necessarily less insightful than strictly musical analysis, whether of the Schenkerian or some other variety, as is evident from the subtle and exhaustive analyses of Schubert songs by Arnold Feil and the late Professor Thrasybulos Georgiades in Germany. In America, unfortunately, the one serious recent study of the German lied is valuable mainly as shock therapy. In *Poem and Music in the German Lied*, the late Jack M. Stein prods all the great nineteenth-century lieder composers for their misreadings of poetry; for example, he dismisses our song on account of its "mood of naiveté and sentimental innocence." There is often something in what Stein says. But while Schumann certainly comes dangerously close to sentimentality in his setting of the word *klingen*, we should also reckon on the clipped and dryly repetitious musical phrase which returns unvaried for "das Lied der Nachtigall." Does this not effectively undercut the sentimental tendency? On this occasion, at least, Schumann has not smoothed away the celebrated irony of his poet.

Komar's criticism of Schenker and Forte as regards the *Ursatz* stems from his reading of the song in conjunction with the preceding member of the cycle, "Im wunderschönen Monat Mai," the beautiful and well-known opening song. He is right as far as he goes, though he does not go so far as to make the obvious point that since "Aus meinen Thränen" follows directly the famous C-sharp-seventh chord on which that opening song is left hanging, its first few notes do not announce an unambiguous A major, as Schenker so brutally assumed, but, rather, for a fleeting moment, the expected resolution in F-sharp minor. So even the first half-prominent gesture in the song, the articulation of *spriessen*, sounds more poetic and less naive, less sentimental, than Stein would have us believe.

Komar says that Schumann forged the two songs "virtually into a single entity" from a strictly musical standpoint. If so, that shows that, unlike his analysts, he cared that the two poems also form a unit:

> Im wunderschönen Monat Mai,
> Als alle Knospen sprangen,
> Da ist in meinen Herzen
> Die Liebe aufgegangen.
>
> Im wunderschönen Monat Mai,
> Als alle Vögel sangen,
> Da hab' ich ihr gestanden
> Mein Sehnen und Verlangen.
>
> Aus meinen Thränen spriessen
> Viel blühende Blumen hervor,
> Und meine Seufzer werden
> Ein Nachtigallenchor.
>
> Und wenn du mich lieb hast, Kindchen,
> Schenk' ich dir die Blumen all',
> Und vor dienem Fenster soll klingen
> Das Lied der Nachtigall.

The *Knospen* of the first song open into *blühende Blumen* in the second, the *Vögel* identify themselves as *Nachtigallen*, and so on. In terms of critical methodology, Komar's emphasis on the cycle's continuity merely transfers his organicist investigation from the level of the song to the higher level of the cycle. Still, there is some value to his procedure in that it indicates a broadening out; one may ask what the real subject of the critic's attention should be—the G-natural that Komar calls the "major analytic issue" of the song, or the total music of the song, or the song's music taken together with its words, or the full sixteen-song *Dichterliebe* cycle. Or perhaps the entire output of Schumann's so-called "song year," 1840. As is well known, *Dichterliebe* was composed along with about 120 other songs in a single burst of creative energy lasting eleven months, a period that encompassed the composer's marriage, after agonizing delays, to Clara Wieck.

All the songs of 1840 were written for Clara, and many of them were written directly to her. *Dichterliebe* begins the same way that Schumann ended his earlier Heine song cycle, op. 24: with a song of dedication. The poet-composer offers his work to his beloved, work that is formed out of his love and his longing. Heretofore, however, Schumann had been transforming his longing not into nightingale songs but into piano pieces. This suggests a new irony to the word *klingen* and a double (or by now a triple) irony if one thinks of the shallow virtuoso pieces by Herz and Pixis on which Clara was making her reputation as a pianist while Robert was attacking them angrily in his journalism, crippling his hand in a mechanism designed to strengthen it, and bit by bit relinquishing his own ambitions as a performer. The sixteen songs now dedicated to Clara speak of love's distress, not of love's happiness. Clara, incidentally, was twelve years old when Robert first turned up as her father's student, already a sick man and a rather alarmingly dissolute one. "Aus meinen Thränen" is the only one of Schumann's love songs which includes the word *Kind* or *Kindchen.*

The comprehensive study of the Schumann songs published ten years ago by the English critic and cryptographer Eric Sams has not been much noticed in the United States. Sams takes a strong contraanalytical line and also puts people off by his somewhat brazen pursuit of a special theory about Schumann's compositional practice. This devolves on the composer's use of a complicated network of private musical symbolism; thus, Sams identifies several secret "Clara themes" in "Aus meinen Thränen," among them the expressive descending-scale figure on the word *Kindchen* mentioned above. The analysts cannot do anything with data of this kind. As far as they are concerned, the same notes in the same musical context ought always to produce the same "sounding form," whether written by Schumann or Schubert or Mendelssohn. But it is not unusual for composers to nurture private musical symbols. Berg is a famous case in point. Schumann is unusual, perhaps, only in the large number of studied clues he left around for future decoders. No doubt Sams goes too far. If what we value in an artist is his individual vision, however, rather than the evidence he brings in support of some general analytical system, we shall certainly want to enter as far as possible into his idiosyncratic world of personal association and imagery.

Looking again, more broadly, at Schumann's songs and the tradition from which they sprang, one must come to a consideration of characteristics inherent in the genre itself. An artistic genre has a life of its own in history; criticism cannot proceed as though history did not exist. The nineteenth-century German lied began with a firm alliance to a romantically conceived *Volksweise,* and while from Schubert on the history of the genre is usually seen in terms of a transcendence of this ideal, composers have never wished to transcend it entirely. Evocations of the *Volkstümlich* were handled excellently, in their different ways, by Beethoven, Schubert, Brahms, and even Wolf, to say nothing of Mahler. But Stein was right: Schumann's evocations are always tinged with "sentimental innocence." Some further examples may be cited: "Volksliedchen," op. 51 no. 2, "Der arme Peter," op. 53 no. 3, "Marien-würmchen," op. 79 no. 14, "Lied eines Schmiedes," op. 90 no. 1, "Mond, meine Seele Liebling," op. 104 no. 1, and "Hoch, hoch sind die Berge," op. 138 no. 8.

Sams makes the same point and also stresses that, in addition to word-cyphers and musical quotations, Schumann was also addicted to disguises, of which the impulsive Florestan and the introspective Eusebius are only the most public—so much so, that in works like *Carnaval* and *Dichterliebe* one sometimes feels impelled to ask the real Robert Schumann to please step forward. In *Dichterliebe*, by contrast with the song cycles of Beethoven and Schubert, many of the songs seem to assume different personae: compare "Aus meinen Thränen" with "Ich grolle nicht," "Wenn ich in deine Augen seh'," "Ich hab' in Traum geweinet," and others. Schumann's self-consciousness as regards the implications of genre and sub-genre must be taken into account for any comprehensive understanding of his artistic intentions.

The term "persona" has been borrowed from literary criticism by a musician whose commitment to analysis has never blinded him to what Cavell calls a "humane criticism of music," Edward T. Cone. In his latest book, *The Composer's Voice*, Cone's argument, which ultimately goes much further than the lied repertory, begins with Schubert's "Erlkönig." He first inquires who it is that sings the various "voices" in this well-known song, and next invites us to distinguish the vocal persona or personae from that of the piano part which underlies and binds the whole together. This seems a fruitful line to take with "Aus meinen Thränen." At first the vocal and instrumental parts run closely parallel, but they pull apart at those ambiguous cadences to which attention was drawn earlier. The voice and the piano stop in their own ways and in their own sweet time; how are we to conceive of their coordination? A highly suggestive question that Cone asks about songs is whether the pianist hears the singer and vice versa (more precisely, whether the instrumental persona hears the vocal persona). There is no doubt that the pianist hears the singer in bar 12 of "Aus meinen Thränen," but I am less sure that he does so in bar 4 and I am fairly sure he does not in bar 17. At this point, the attention of the instrumental persona is directed elsewhere, toward some arcane and fascinating musical thought-process of his own.

Can analysis help us here? Cone likes to address his musical criticism to musical performance, and I believe that a resolution of this question of the vocal and instrumental personae will also resolve one performance problem with this small, fragile, and haunting song: namely, the treatment of the fermatas in bars 4, 8, and 16.

It should be understood that the alternatives suggested above to traditional musical analysis—in this case, to Schenkerian and post-Schenkerian analysis—are not intended to exhaust the possibilities. They are merely examples of some lines along which a more comprehensive, "humane" criticism of music can and should be developed. Nor is the term "alternative" to be taken in an exclusive sense. One cannot envisage any one or any combination of these alternative modes of criticism as supplanting analysis; they should be joined to analysis to provide a less one-dimensional account of what music is and does. What is important is to find ways of dealing responsibly with other kinds of aesthetic value in music besides organicism. In any case, I cannot envisage traditional analysis continuing for long in its pure form.

As mentioned above, there are a number of pressures today leading to a new breadth and flexibility in academic music criticism. Of these, one of the more powerful emerges from efforts to come to terms with the newest music. The position of Robert Morgan, for example, seems close to that outlined in the present paper, though certainly he formulates that position differently. Morgan feels that the traditional concept of analysis as "the elucidation of a sort of teleological organism"—the language is derived from Cone—must be made broader; the analysis of new music "must examine the composer's intentions in relation to their compositional realization, must discuss the implications of the compositional system in regard to the music it generates, consider how the resulting music relates to older music and to other present-day music, examine its perceptual problems, etc. There is really no end to the possibilities that could enable this list to be extended." Indeed, "a pressing responsibility of present-day analysis is to indicate how new music reflects present-day actuality."[12]

Within the narrow confines of the music-academic community, this call for analysis to examine, discuss, and indicate what it never thought of examining, discussing, or indicating before may well prove to be perplexing. Without, the only thing that will perplex is Morgan's clinging to the term "analysis." What he seems clearly to be talking about is criticism, and he is talking about it in a way that must surely enlist sympathy.

Notes

1. Stanley Cavell, *Must We Mean What We Say?* (New York: Scribner's, 1969), p. 182.

2. Ibid., p. 185.

3. I must now [1981] except Cone, who brings criticism and analysis together in an important comprehensive essay, "The Authority of Music Criticism," *Journal of the American Musicological Society* 34 (1981): 1-18.

4. "A Profile for American Musicology," *Journal of the American Musicological Society* 18 (1965): 65.

5. *The Bach Reader*, ed. Hans T. David and Arthur Mendel (New York: Norton, 1945), pp. 352-53.

6. Cavell, *Must We Mean What We Say?*, p. 186.

7. "Work . . . by 'one-off' analysts like Rosen or Kerman [is] frequently held to be suspect in its theoretical focus," writes Jonathan M. Dunsby in *Journal of the Arnold Schoenberg Institute* 3 (1979): 195. "They seem to embed the most penetrating and original insight about specific musical objects in an all-embracing cultural critique that can be ultimately confusing, without the deep-rooted convictions —often hard to live with but always comprehensible—of the Schoenbergian analytical tradition."

8. "Grammatical Simplicity and Relational Richness: The Trio of Mozart's G Minor Symphony," *Critical Inquiry* 2, no. 4 (1976): 693-761.

9. Another widely discussed new analyst, David Epstein, prefaces his book *Beyond Orpheus* (Cambridge, Mass.: MIT Press, 1979) with this statement about "the limitations imposed on the [analytical] studies that follow. First, they are concerned with music written within the era commonly known as classic-romantic, in effect from Haydn and Mozart through the middle of the nineteenth century, as delimited by Brahms. Secondly, these studies are restricted to music written in what might be called the German-Viennese tradition—the most seminal body of music that emerged during this broad period. Third, they are confined to absolute music. . . . A fourth and final limitation: The matter of 'expression' in music is beyond the confines of these studies." One hears the sound of windows closing.

10. Arthur Komar, ed. *Robert Schumann: Dichterliebe* (Norton Critical Score) (New York: Norton, 1971), p. 70-71. "Schenker's Conception of Musical Structure," one of Allen Forte's earlier articles, first appeared in *Journal of Music Theory* 3 (1959): 1-30 and has since been reprinted in Komar's casebook, pp. 96-106, and as the first item in *Readings in Schenker Analysis and Other Approaches*, ed. Maury Yeston (New Haven: Yale University Press, 1977), pp. 3-37. In a graded list of "Initial Readings in Schenker" prepared by another leading analyst, Richmond Browne, for *In Theory Only* 1 (1975): 4, Forte's article appears as the second item from the top.

11. Reprinted by permission from Heinrich Schenker, *Free Composition (Der Freie Satz)*, ed. and trans. Ernst Oster, 2 vols. (New York: Longman, 1979), vol. 2, fig. 21b.

12. "On the Analysis of Recent Music," *Critical Inquiry* 4 (1977): 40, 51.

4

Understanding Music

MONROE C. BEARDSLEY

WHETHER THERE IS MORE TO MUSIC than meets the ear has been a persistent, or at least recurrent, question since classical times—though to lift the dispute to a fruitful level of clarity we must abandon this crudely convenient way of stating it. Of course, there is more to music than tickling or battering by sound waves, if only because perception involves more of the organism than the ear. But, however much we crowd into our theory of perception, under the guidance of the cognitive psychologists, there will be at least the potentiality of discovering more about an object or event than what we perceive in it. We perceive a tree: do we thereby *understand* it? It seems that "perception" and "understanding" are in a way complementary terms, and perhaps together they cover the central cognition of an object. There is certainly more to the tree than what we perceive—but when we have *both* perceived and understood (although we have by no means answered all the questions that could be asked about the tree, such as where it is and what will become of it), we can be said to *know* the tree as an object, to apprehend its nature.

What, then, is understanding? You will, I hope, applaud my resolution to rein in this question so that it does not run away with us into distant fields of philosophy. Still, it has to be asked, and some answer, however sketchy, has to be attempted if we are to make a propitious start. We might distinguish many kinds of understanding, but all of them, I think, can be encompassed by three basic categories, each of which has its own corresponding form of *mis*understanding and of *un*understanding.

1. *Causal* (or *genetic*) understanding consists in knowing under what conditions and in what way the object had to become what it is. Thus, a person who complains that he does not understand trees may be comforted if he is shown what makes trees

I am indebted to James Harris, Ronald Hathaway, and David Greene for very thoughtful comments on this essay.

germinate and grow. Some philosophers would wish to insert here, as a second category, purposive or teleological understanding—not that it applies to a tree (unless you are an Aristotelian), but as it might be applied to a machine, which we say we understand when we know what function it was designed to fulfill. But I include the intentions and purposes of machine-makers under causal conditions, broadly considered, and so do not require a special category for them.

2. *Configurational* understanding consists in knowing how the details, the elements and subordinate parts, of an object fit into a pattern or structure that characterizes the whole. It is grasping the anatomy and physiology of the tree, seeing how it is organized and how its differentiated organs work together. Thus, a person who admits that he does not understand why some trees shed their bark or exude gum will be helped if we show him how these features or processes have configurational significance in relation to other features or processes, and make their contribution to the life and character of the tree.

Some philosophers might wish to provide a category for rule-understanding here, as when we speak of understanding how to play pinochle or of understanding what is going on in a game of pinochle we happen to be observing; but this kind of understanding can be subsumed under the second category, I believe. It is still an overall configuration—a system—we aim to grasp, so that we can understand how the particular moves are related to it.

3. *Semantic* understanding consists in knowing what something signifies (taking this term in a comprehensive sense). The tree, evidently, will not serve to illustrate this form of understanding—not, at any rate, if it is just any old tree. One could *plant* a tree with proper ceremonies that would give it a meaning (it may signify, for example, the class of 1979's wishes for the long life of its alma mater), and it could then be interpreted in this third fashion as a kind of message. In a similar way, a wink, at the right moment, can be semantically understood—or misunderstood.

It is well to be warned from the start that configurational and semantic understanding are readily and often confounded. That troublesome word "meaning" —which we are reluctant to scold because its mischief results from its very eagerness to be serviceable in all sorts of contexts—is also often applied to configurational connections. We can say we understand the meaning of a lever or push-button in the nuclear plant's control room when we learn that it opens a valve in the cooling system (or, at any rate, that's what it's supposed to do). Still, the word "meaning" here refers to function or role, not meaning in the semantic sense; the lever does not serve as sign or symbol, like the label under it, but as a means to an end. Similarly, to speak of the "harmonic meaning" of a particular note in a music-work is to speak of a configurational connection.

Labored as they may be, these preliminary distinctions can help us to pin down the exact locus of the problem about music that is to occupy our attention. The musical work, like the tree, plainly lends itself (or at least submits itself) to the first two forms of understanding, so there is no serious dispute about them. We can try to understand it causally in the manner of the music historian, for presumably some antecedent conditions and influences, social and psychological, had something to do with its becoming. Or we can try to understand it configurationally, by seeing how its parts, its subordinate events and relationships, fit into a larger pattern. It is this latter form of understanding with which Joseph Kerman is almost wholly concerned in his essay "The State of Academic Music Criticism." Its most prominent species these days is, as he points out, music analysis. And if music analysis is to be conceived as "the technical demonstration of the coherence of individual pieces of music,"[1] it is *only* a species, for the analytical examination of a music-work may also serve, as with Leonard Meyer, to demonstrate the *complexity* of the work or, as Kerman suggests in discussing Schumann's "Aus meinen Thränen," its "emotional temperature"[2]—by which I believe he refers to what I would call the intensity of its human regional qualities. Speaking of the piano phrases marking the ends of lines 2, 4, and 8 of the poem, Kerman writes: "How are these rather haunting, contradictory stops to be understood (or 'heard,' as musicians like to say) at the two points within the body of the song? And how are they to be heard at the end?"[3] In other words, How do they contribute to the overall character of the combined word-music-work?

Apart from these two forms of understanding, is the music-work like a tree (the one that grows anyhow, not the one dedicated at commencement), in that it has nothing in the way of a signification to be apprehended or pointed out? Or is it like a poem, say, which presumably does signify something and solicits our understanding (and sometimes rewards it)?

The differences among these three forms of understanding can be sharpened by a familiar musical example: Smetana's String Quartet in E Minor, and particularly one notable even in this work, the sudden, sustained E, three octaves above middle C, in the finale (bars 224-30).

A configurational understanding of this event would involve (at least in part) seeing how this note sharply alters the mood and appropriately introduces a coda in which earlier themes are briefly recalled before the quartet ends very quietly with E-major chords. It might also involve recognizing that this note, however unexpected,. is prepared for by sequences of somewhat grotesque leaps to high notes earlier in the quartet[4]—leaps that create strained intensities, though never reaching the high E.

A semantic understanding of this event might involve taking the notes as referring to the last tone that sounded in the composer's ear just before his deafness, and perhaps via this reference, as symbolizing the blows of fate, the bludgeonings of chance.

A causal understanding of this musical event might involve a grasp of the composer's actual intention: that in writing this note he wished to refer to or symbolize something, or believed himself to be referring or symbolizing—and/or that he aimed to compose a coda that is dramatic but connected organically with the rest of the work.

Now there is room for some dispute about the applicability of semantic understanding to this quartet: some philosophers would deny that Smetana *could* make his high E refer to an event in his life, however significant to him, or make it symbolize the blows of fate, however much he suffered under them. I have been inclined in this direction myself, but on balance I do not favor it. Smetana, after all, did give a subtitle to his work—"From My Life"—and thereby invited us to look for parallels, and (I think) to take striking parallels (as between the high E in the work and the high E in his life) as references. Moreover, in his letter of 12 April 1878, he wrote that his aim in composing this quartet (that is, one of his intentions) was to represent the course of his life; and he provided a sketchy program for the work assigning each movement to a stage of that life.[5] If *anything* can give this sort of meaning to this string quartet, it seems to me that Smetana has succeeded in doing so.

Notice that I do *not* say that Smetana could make the note refer to an event in his life merely by casually remarking that it does. The establishment of reference requires rather more than a fiat. Loosely speaking, we may say that it calls for appeal to a *rule* of reference—either to a rule already in force, agreed upon by the parties involved (the composer and those who hear his work), or to a new rule explicitly laid down for the occasion under conditions that make the rule acceptable. A composer who provides a program for his work may be said to have legitimately proposed such rules, and hence to have established the particular references covered by the rules. So much, I think, we should be willing to concede. (But this concession does not justify such nonsense as Leonard Bernstein's television remarks taking the kettledrum beats in the first movement of Mahler's Ninth Symphony as referring to Mahler's irregular heartbeat that presaged his death.)

You see that I have not been willing to go along with philosophers who would hold, along with Richard Kuhns, that Smetana's quartet "expresses thought about his deafness with the introduction of a specific note."[6] Working into his quartet an allusion to his deafness, by providing verbal clues, is one thing; but working opinions about deafness into the quartet seems a good deal more of a feat. The kind of meaning, then, that we have so far illustrated is limited indeed, so it may be well to provide ourselves with examples of more interesting claims that have been made for the semantic understanding of music.

Consider, first, Olivier Messiaen's statement: "I want to write music that is an act of faith, a music that is about everything without ceasing to be about God." Allen Hughes begins an article on Messiaen with this quotation and ends with the words: "His music is essentially a music of meditation. Messiaen is a composer with something special to say."[7] And, by way of contrast, consider a Russian critic writing of Shostakovich's Fourteenth Symphony: "He wants to exalt life and its blessing and therefore denounces death as the worst evil, railing against it with characteristic passion. Those who have heard the symphony understand that in Shostakovich's handling of the death theme there is a complete lack of pretense at contempt, of mystical dread and curiosity."[8] In such remarks, something more than biographical allusions are broached; some portions of Christian doctrine and of dialectical materialism are found in this music-work.

But how *can* music—without accompanying words—convey such ideas? That is the ever-recurring question. For these composers and critics do not claim that their words have *assigned* or *given* a signification to the music, I suppose: they are telling us how they semantically understand the work and how it is to be semantically understood. To justify claims of this sort requires a theory of musical signification, in terms of which particular works can be interpreted. So it is appropriate to take a brief look at some well-known and forthright attempts over the past twenty years to provide such a theory and thus make possible and intelligible the semantical understanding of music.

Before coming to these proposals, however, we should remind ourselves of a very fundamental distinction between two ways of talking about music; for much mischief, I think, has come from overlooking their differences. A clear example of one of these ways of talking is provided by the discussion, in a recent book by David Epstein, of Mahler's scherzi (for example, in the First and Fifth symphonies): "Waltzes initially introduced in the most elegant Viennese manner are transformed into visions of the demonic—bitter, ironic caricatures of their former selves. Tempi increased almost to headlong rushings; elegant articulations turn into harsh and heavy accents; sweet, characteristic waltz harmonies give way to bizarre dissonances; stateliness and control move toward disorganization and chaos. The music at its height seems an analogue of a schizoid, if not paranoid, state."[9] Now, as we know, there is a school of contemporary music theorists (a number of them associated with the periodical *Perspectives of New Music*) that disdains to talk about music in this way—although the passage is, I think, a reasonable sample (well, perhaps a bit exaggerated) of the way people have talked about music since ancient times. For example, Benjamin Boretz has written about the custom of calling some music "sad":

> And in this light, the only problem with 'sad' is that we simply have nothing observational to tie it to in either music or painting, and so it makes no difference to the music or painting-identity of anything. In use, however, such "proper names" have *negative* value, since they serve to perpetuate the internalization of a perceiver's theoretical scheme and, hence, to minimize his competence. The world of the average listener contains very little music and a great deal of noise, a gap which he tends to cover by the invocation of picturesque place-holding slogans.
>
> But to a sophisticated observer, the space thus straddled is filled with so many determinate particulars producing such particular identities that the sloganizing terms actually do seem hopelessly inapplicable. Like prescientific attributions, to natural phenomena, of anthropomorphic and volitional characteristics, predictions like 'sad' of art simply symptomatize an underprivileged *stage* of cognition, not a *category* thereof.[10]

It seems to me that two important epistemological distinctions are slurred here. First, it may be false to say that a tree literally longs to embrace the sunlight, instead of saying that it exhibits tropism. But to say, metaphorically, that the tree is stalwart may nevertheless register a true phenomenological discovery—and the same can be said of describing music as demonic, or angelic. Second, smelling the tree's blossoms does not provide a grasp of its organic chemistry, and hearing the "headlong rushings" of Mahler does not bring with it configurational understanding. Nevertheless, whether we call such perceptions a "stage" or a "category" of cognition, they are still cognitions. We know something our ears have told us, and something worth knowing, when we know that the Mahler scherzo is bitter, ironic, harsh—rather than elegant, stately, sweet. Nothing in Boretz's argument proves that these predicates are really "inapplicable."

But now I have come into conflict with Karl Aschenbrenner, who holds that remarks such as those I have quoted from David Epstein are not genuine descriptions at all, and in fact are neither true nor false. He calls them "characterizations," in a special sense, and says they may be more or less "apt" or "telling," but they lack truth value. This view is developed in his recent book[11] and summarized in his lecture "Music Criticism: Practice and Malpractice." He says: "I may regard some musical subject as strident and cacophonous, or as being artificial, 'bloodless, paper music.' In these cases I think it is an error to suppose that such remarks are either objectively true or false."[12] I confess that I find this position difficult to grasp. How can Aschenbrenner regard a musical subject as strident except by believing (however tentatively) that it *is* strident? And how can he believe a proposition without thinking it is true? How can a remark about music be "apt" or "telling" unless it somehow correctly (i.e., truly) ascribes some property to the music that the music actually has? And how can characterizations support what he calls "commendations" (e.g., "This music is good"), unless they are capable of entering into logical structures involving relations among truth values?[13] Take Aschenbrenner's list of other adjectives metaphorically applied to music: how could they be "used by critics to draw our attention to something in music or the other arts which in listening or watching we may have overlooked,"[14] if they could not be truly predicated of those works? The stridency of a musical passage belongs to it as much as does any other property of it.

But I promised to introduce a more fundamental distinction between two ways of talking about music, and so far I have only defended the legitimacy of one kind of talk—that which is so well illustrated by Epstein. The other kind consists in what Epstein does *not* say, which is equally noteworthy. He does speak of "visions of the demonic," but not as something somehow represented by Mahler, rather as something into which the waltzes are "transformed"; so I take him to be describing the music itself as demonic. He ends by observing that the music "seems an analogue" of a psychotic state, uncertainty diagnosed: but he does not add that the music *refers* to such a state, or is *about* such a state, or *says* something about that state. He does not, in short, assume or imply that the music has a signification, but only that it has certain qualities, which we may, if we like, compare with the qualities of other things. Those musical qualities that do notably resemble qualities of human beings, or their states of mind, traits, actions, or activities, we may conveniently call "human qualities"—the music is schizoid or it rushes headlong. It is this distinction I wish to emphasize and rely on as we proceed: between *describing* music as having certain human qualities and *interpreting* music as signifying or referring to the things they resemble. And although—or perhaps just because—such concepts as 'signifying' and 'meaning' are highly flexible and variable, I shall focus on the concept of reference. Granted that music may be bitter; in being so, does it refer to something external to itself, as Messiaen and Shostakovich, and their supportive music critics, evidently claim?

Rose Subotnik's essay "Romantic Music as Post-Kantian Critique," despite its many illuminations, seems to me to take some unearned advantage from a blurring of this distinction. It may be, as she claims, that classical music is a "semiotic structure" and that classical works "propose the . . . ideal of the . . . universe . . . as an autonomous intelligible whole;"[15] but to demonstrate this it is not enough merely to show that the music is in some respects analogous to a logical structure. And if we regard the intramusical relations in a classical work (those relations we study for configurational understanding) as semiotic, that does not automatically give the work the *external* semiotic relations that call for semantic understanding. Again, she remarks that "Together, the chromatic and pianistic sonorities of Chopin's Prelude in A Minor, along with the relentlessness of ostinato rhythm and the percussiveness of the constant pianistic attack on pairs of low-pitched notes, give this piece the meaning that is almost surely the one most often attached to it—its character of harshness as a total configuration."[16] But meaning and character ought not to be treated as the same. Much confusion in musical aesthetics would be avoided by a resolution to stick to a stricter use of "meaning."

The first of the four books I think we should take a look at is *The Language of Music*, by Deryck Cooke. His thesis is that "music is a language of the emotions,"[17] and his aim is to lay the "foundations" of a more comprehensive theory and thereby "make it ultimately possible to understand and assess a composer's work as a report on human experience."[18] The demonstration of the thesis consists in a remarkable set of classified melodic figures, ranging over the entire history of Western music, which are supposed to reveal "the elements of musical expression, or the basic terms of musical vocabulary." Now, one might think that the way to show that music is a language of the emotions would be to explain the rules of reference that govern various kinds of musical happening—rules that would enable the composer, in writing music, to "report on" the emotions. It is possible that Cooke thought he was doing something of the sort, but in fact he never does. There is constant resort to the verb "express," whose ambiguity serves to hide the basic distinction between *referring* to an emotion and merely *possessing* a quality that can be metaphorically described by an emotion-word.

Thus, to mention but two of the many musical idioms so plentifully illustrated by Cooke, "a phrase of two notes (the minor sixth of the scale falling to the fifth) is to be found expressing anguish in music" by composers from Josquin to Britten;[19] and in a "triadic context the major third expresses a feeling of settled, enduring pleasure, the minor third a feeling of settled, enduring pain."[20] What the accumulated evidence shows is that each of these melodic figures can contribute or intensify a *quality* of anguish or pleasantness in a perhaps surprising variety of musical contexts. The evidence does not show that there is expressing in a sense that involves referring, directing our attention, to emotions—except, of course, where the music is accompanied by words. Hundreds of examples, interesting as they are in themselves, establish reference no more than a single one, and fail to justify such a conclusion as this: "If Bach, for example, began the slow movement of his Two-Violin Concerto in D Minor with the major 8-7-6-5, he must have meant to express a feeling of joy welcomed and received as comfort or consolation; and if Beethoven used the same term to open the slow movement of his Fourth Symphony, and Brahms to open the slow movement of his First Piano Concerto, they too must have meant to express the same feeling."[21] If all three composers "must have meant to express the same feeling," they must have been able to refer to the same feeling by the same melodic figure; but to show that this can be done it is not enough, as Cooke thinks, merely to show that all three passages have similar human qualities.

Some readers will no doubt consider it a waste of time to point out the failures of *The Language of Music*. But the examples are impressive and have swayed even quite careful readers. And the basic mistake—that of jumping from the notion of the music's *being* sad to the notion of the music's *referring* to sad states of mind—is worth reminding ourselves of, though it has quite often been made and sometimes caught and reproved.

The second book is Donald N. Ferguson's *Music as Metaphor*, which aims "to describe both the manner in which the musical substance functions for expressions and also the product of that functioning," on the principle that "expressiveness inevitably implies reference to non-musical experience."[22] Expression, "in the proper sense of the word, . . . is the *intelligible* utterance, not merely of feeling but of thought."[23] "To establish expressive meaning as resident in music will therefore be to demonstrate that this art, like the others, has essential relation to non-artistic experience, and so to truth."[24] Ferguson's theory is elaborately developed, but the gist of it can be not unfairly abstracted. Ferguson holds that every emotion has three elements: a stimulus or contextual concept (e.g., a charging tiger), a particular kind of tension, and a disposition to motor activity (e.g., to run). Music possesses the means to imitate two of these factors: its tonal tension is like emotional tension, and its "ideal motion" is like motor activity. Through these two resources it can "portray" or "represent" an emotion by supplying a particular sort of tension and of motion, inducing the listener himself to infer a suitable contextual concept.[25] When we listen to the passacaglia theme in the slow movement of Bach's keyboard Concerto in D Minor, we must say, "Surely these are the tensions and the consequent imaginal motor impulses of a spirit in travail?"[26]

Let us agree with two of Ferguson's points: that we do hear in this music a kind of tension that can also be felt in spiritual travail, and that the music moves in a way we might expect a person in spiritual travail to move. Are we then authorized to take his third step and say that the music *refers* to spiritual travail? Well, what more can be asked? you might wonder. Just this: the music's tension and motion can also be felt in an indefinite variety of other forms of travail, trial, and tribulation. In order to make good a reference to a particular *kind* of mental state, the music itself must supply the concept directing our attention to that kind of state—and this is exactly what Ferguson concedes that the music (apart from the words that Bach later set to it) cannot do. Hanslick made this point long ago. If I may be permitted an example from the extreme of absurdity, Ferguson's view is like saying that you could play for someone who never watches television the music of one of McDonald's commercials and expect him (with no aid from words) to recognize, from its special tension and ideal motion, that it celebrates the glories of quick-served hamburgers. But, you may reply with some asperity, that is just the difference in genius between the two composers. Or, you may say, that is just the difference between spiritual travail and an enthusiasm for Big Macs. I do not deny either difference; I only insist that Ferguson's procedure for achieving semantic understanding of music is unworkable, because it leads to no definite reference, but only to a multiple ambiguity.

The third book I want to discuss is *The Musical Symbol*, by Gordon Epperson. Symbols, he holds, "contain elements of what they stand for. . . . The symbolic in music . . . is that quality which speaks . . . to the human percipient . . . and awakens an echo, a recognition, within him."[27] Epperson says many interesting things, but his argument consists largely in a historical account of various philosophic views, and there is no effort to establish musical reference. It seems indeed, that Epperson thinks that his view of symbolism somehow by-passes the need for reference. He says that "some essence, as it were, of the life of feeling is objectified in the aural image and freed from the demands of the immediate. It becomes then an object of contemplation; it is meaningful for the psyche: it has relevance, in a formal and concentrated way, to life in its generality."[28] The first part of this passage excites no dispute; but the nature of the final "relevance" is precisely what needs to be explained and justified. A symbol must do more than just *be* something; it must symbolize something, and that requires a semantic relation.

The fourth book is Wilson Coker's *Music and Meaning*, which does make an admirably systematic attempt to furnish a theory of musical meaning and a broad, well-illustrated survey of its major types. Coker has an especially good section on the varieties of musical motion.[29] Music he holds to be a sign or a structure of signs.[30] It consists of "musical gestures"[31] that can "signify" many kinds of things external to music itself and thus have "extrageneric musical meaning."[32] Such gestures "readily provide metaphors significant of, and comparable to, affective and conative states that we know by experience."[33]

Comparability is not in question, but signification is, so we turn with interest to Coker's basic account of signs in general. We find that his account is taken over from Charles Morris, with all the defects and deficiencies that have long been recognized in that view. "Whatever acts as a sign in some way or ways causes an interpreter to take account of an object or event."[34] But what is it to "take account of"? "Subjectively, something (A) is a sign of something else (B) if an organism (O) behaves in the presence of A in a manner appropriate to B. Objectively, something (A) is a sign of something else (B) if and only if in fact A accompanies, follows, or refers back to B."[35] Neither the objective account nor the subjective account applies literally and generally to music. The objective account is certainly very broad; it entails, for example, that if Jones regularly breaks out in a rash after eating turnips, the rash is a sign of Jones's turnip-eating. But is there anything that Bach's passacaglia theme follows as the rash the turnip? The subjective account serves well for the sense in which the sign *"Beware! Vicious Dog!"* serves to signify; no doubt it will induce avoidance behavior similar to what would be "appropriate" to the presence of the beast itself. But the subjective account hardly seems to encompass a painting of a bulldog in an art gallery (How is our behavior there suitable for encountering an actual dog?) or a song about Old Dog Tray. If Bach's passacaglia theme signifies spiritual travail, it is surely not because hearing the theme makes us behave "in a manner appropriate" to spiritual travail.

So I conclude that Wilson Coker succeeds no better than his predecessors in explaining how muscial works can refer beyond themselves and can thus call for semantic understanding.

I have set aside here another kind of reference, on which Charles Rosen's essay "Influence: Plagiarism and Inspiration" casts much light. Taking "influence" as the most general causal term in the history of the arts, Rosen raises the problem of how to distinguish between artistic influence that does not involve reference and artistic influence that does: between betrayal of influence and outright allusion, between borrowing and plagiarism, between resemblance and imitation. He distinguishes usefully between "structural" and "thematic" musical quotation: Brahms's opening of his B-flat Concerto with a cadenza versus Brahms's inclusion of an ornamented version of Beethoven's *Emperor* theme—"a magnificent homage." Musical quotation consists in using a musical element in a way that preseves recognizable identity and yet naturalizes or assimilates it—the combination is hard to describe and needs study.[36] Reference is generated by the work itself, given its position in music history, not by the composer's intention. Thus, I question the suggestion at the end of Rosen's essay that it is Brahms's awareness of the particular similarity of his violin concerto to Beethoven's G-Major Piano Concerto that makes the similarity a reference.[37] Truer, I think, is his remark: "The two open references to Beethoven's *Emperor* Concerto made by Brahms's Piano Concerto no. 2 in B-flat Major are placed in such crucial places, so set in relief, in fact, that they must be understood as staking a claim. This work, we are informed by these open references, is intended to follow upon the tradition left off by Beethoven."[38] The setting-in-relief does indeed establish reference. Whether it also makes the concerto claim so much is a harder question, but on reflection I am inclined to agree with Rosen's interpretation, though it is not easy to show philosophically that such interpretations can be reasonable. More doubtful, perhaps, is the further remark, about the thematic allusion, that "it also acknowledges the existence of a previous classical style, an aspiration to re-create it, and an affirmation that such a recreation is no longer possible on naive or independent terms."[39] That is a great deal for a musical allusion to say.

Against this background, we must look at a rather different approach to our problem undertaken by Nelson Goodman in his enormously valuable book *Languages of Art*.[40] Though he takes "refer" as an undefined term, he gives us some help in grasping its meaning in his system (partly by examples, partly by discussion), and he does much to articulate the specific kind of reference that, in his view, plays a major role in music. This is "exemplification," and it is defined as follows: Predicates are expressions of the form "is blue" and "drives a car"; when they are properly combined with logical subjects, they become sentences that are true or false. So we have "Jones's car is blue." If this is true, we can say that the predicate "is blue"

applies to Jones's car or that it denotes Jones's car (among many other things). Now suppose that Jones's car is denoted by a certain predicate and also refers to the predicate that denotes it; then Jones's car exemplifies that predicate. Although, strictly speaking, Goodman holds that it is predicates (and nonverbal labels) that are exemplified, he reluctantly allows a more comfortable idiom in which it is *properties* (such as the property of being blue or of driving a car) that are exemplified.

But how can this be? Jones's car *is* blue, but hardly refers to its own property. Well, exemplifying is what examples do. Suppose we are discussing mispronunciation, and you cite the word "nuclear" as one that is frequently mispronounced—as in "nucular families" and "nucular power plants." Then you are using the word "nuclear" to illustrate one of its properties (the property of being frequently mispronounced). It then exemplifies that property (at least on that occasion). But also, be it noted, I am using the case of the word "nuclear"'s being an example of a word frequently mispronounced to exemplify exemplification itself—that is, the property of exemplifying.

This is just what music-works, along with other art-works, do with some of their qualities, according to Goodman. They refer to them when they "display," or "show forth," or "exhibit," or "feature" these qualities. The semantic understanding of a sonata, then, involves discerning which of its heard qualities are thus exemplified.

An attractive and coherent theory, even in the condensed form in which I have stated it! Perhaps the first thing to note about it is the way its strength derives, in part, from its self-restraint. For it attempts to sustain one of the main claims of the theories we have just considered—namely, that music is referential—by abandoning their other main claim—namely, that music refers to objects, events, and states of affairs in the world outside music. On Goodman's theory, it is only *properties* that can be referred to in this exemplificational manner (if we set aside the alternative formulation in terms of predicates and other labels). So Goodman's theory will not justify our saying that Messiaen's music refers to God or Shostakovich's symphony to life and death or Smetana's high E to an experience in his life.

Yet even so, there are problems with applying the concept of exemplification widely to music and its qualities. Some of these I have discussed on other occasions.[41] They have made me slow to accept a general semiotic theory of the arts, even in its most elegant and compelling version so far. But I have come to understand the exemplification theory better and to appreciate its reasonableness—at least with some qualifications, which I propose to explain.

Let us examine the concept of displaying a little more closely and ask the question: Does displaying always involve, or amount to, referring? When the artfully cosmeticized model moves in her quasi-dance at the fashion show, she displays the clothes she wears, shows them off. In this first sense of the word, it is *persons* who display an object or event. We may call it "object-displaying"—the grocer setting out his fresh strawberries, the rare book librarian putting his precious illuminated manuscript in a glass case. But we can also say that the model's *clothes* themselves display certain significant qualities that mark the new line just arrived from the famous designer: the "trim severe look" or the "loose-billowy look." In this second sense it is the object or event that displays some of its properties; we may call it "property-displaying." The clothes are there on the model precisely to provide examples of the designer's current style.

Now these two modes of displaying can be independent of each other. However unlikely this may be, the model might display clothes that have nothing in the way of significant looks to commend them, so no property-displaying occurs. On the other hand, a tree may display its majestic height and spread even though it happens that no one is displaying the tree. And this contrast suggests an interesting general principle: property-displaying is, or involves, reference when, and only when the property-displaying object is itself object-displayed. The model's garment does indeed refer to (and hence exemplify) those of its properties that are worthy of note under the circumstances, because the garment is itself displayed. But the tree does *not* refer to its properties, however aesthetically noteworthy, because it has not itself been placed on display. What it does is stand there, enabling us to contemplate and enjoy its visible majesty in an aesthetic way. And when Wordsworth, in his famous sonnet, says, "The city now doth like a garment wear / The beauty of the morning," he is saying that London is displaying its beauty ("Earth has not anything to show more fair"), but since the sleeping city is not itself on display—the speaker just happens upon the view—there is no implication that London *refers* to beauty or majesty. So, too, we may add, when Jones's car was in the showroom, before he bought it, it exemplified its special blueness as well as other properties; but later, parked in his driveway, it merely *is* blue.

What follows when we apply this principle to music? Here it seems that we have, or at least usually have, a situation closer to that of the fashion model's clothes than to that of the tree. For in the usual case the music is performed, and under circumstances designed to call attention to it and draw attention away from other things. There is a complication here that I should mention in order to set it aside: by inviting comparison with other performers of the same work—say, Beethoven's Piano Sonata in A Major op. 101—the concert pianist places himself in a competitive situation where he is displaying his own pianistic talents. This competitiveness is one of the main reasons why Glenn Gould has renounced public performances for the making of recordings.[42] But let us focus on the musical aspects of the situation. In playing opus 101, the pianist displays that work and thereby enables the sonata to display some of its qualities; so by our principles, since there is object-displaying, the sonata's own property-displaying amounts to reference (and hence to exemplification). It seems that Goodman's theory fits the case and explains how music in fact refers. Moreover, it enables us to give a semantic dimension to works of other arts, whether or not they are representational, for hanging a picture and publishing a poem can also be regarded as ways of displaying.

So far, we have seen how a music-work can refer to, and thus exemplify, at least some of its properties. But of course, it will never exemplify all of them. This will be true even if we introduce an important restriction. We must distinguish between the sonata and particular performances of it: by Schnabel, Serkin, Brendel, Rosen, Backhaus. If the pianist accidentally plays a C rather than a C-sharp in the first measure, that is a property of his performance, but it is not a property of opus 101. There is a disagreement about the best way to make this distinction, but I think we may take it as indispensable, in some form or other. After we have made it, however, we are still left with an indefinitely large set of properties of the sonata itself, and not all of these are displayed, and so exemplified. Which are and which are not? This is a most serious problem for the exemplification theory.

The question calls for a *general* answer, a principle that will enable us, whichever work may be in question, to determine the exemplified properties so that we may pay proper attention to them and take them into account in judging the work, if we wish to do so. No simple formula will work. For example, we would not want to say that a sonata refers to its most obvious or most prominent features, for it would seem that some of the more subtle ones might have as good a claim to be regarded as exemplified.

The solution of the problem is suggested by our example of the fashion model — or by any other case of displaying, giving samples or examples, that may come to mind. The model's make up may be a striking thing about her when she appears in evening garb that somehow combines lounging pajamas, a nun's habit, and a jump suit. But she is not modeling make up, so the properties of the make-up are not referred to on that occasion, though a rather subtle novelty in the cut of the sleeve *is* referred to. The understood rules of the fashion show establish the distinction: the exemplified properties are those that have some relation to overall purpose or function of fashion shows because they are elements of style in clothing; they mark a borrowing from a style or a deviation from a style. No doubt the matter is a good deal more complex than what my very limited knowledge of fashion shows enables me to say, but I think my main suggestion is right: the principle of exemplification for fashion shows is embedded in the practice itself. And I suggest that the same holds true, *mutatis mutandis*, for the practice of performing piano sonatas. Recalling a phrase I used without emphasis earlier, the properties of the sonata that are exemplified by the sonata are just those properties which are *worthy of note* in the context of concert-giving and concert-going (and recording, too): that is, they are those properties whose presence or absence, or degree of presence, have a direct bearing on the sonata's capacity to interest us aesthetically. They may or may not be of special concern to musicologists or music analysts, but they are qualities to attend to if you are taking the aesthetic point of view. The first movement of opus 101 is in the key of A, with few and restricted modulations; that is a property, but, by itself, it neither enhances nor inhibits the aesthetic satisfactoriness of the sonata. Therefore it is not exemplified. On the other hand, the first movement is unusually hesitant, diffident, indecisive in character; this is a quality that can be enjoyed in it, and (as we shall see shortly) it is a feature that plays an essential role in the marvelous course of the whole sonata. Therefore, it is exemplified. I do not, of course, claim that the principle will always effect a sharp and conclusive disjunction; there will be properties of which we remain uncertain whether they are exemplified. But it gives us guidance and marks out an area — a carefully controlled area — for the semantic understanding of music.

At this stage of the discussion, I have moved beyond Nelson Goodman's published views on these problems, and probably beyond what he would wish to embrace. I cannot regard the exemplification theory as satisfactory or as reasonably complete unless it is supplemented by some general criterion for distinguishing between ex- emplified and nonexemplified properties of music-works, and I can think of no better principle than the one I have tried to articulate—though much more defense is certainly in order. There is a further consequence I think we must draw, and I hope it helps toward an ultimate resolution of the old conflict I alluded to at the beginning, conflict over the possibility, limits, and importance of the semantic understanding of music.

As I have set things up, the distinction between exemplified and nonexemplified qualities depends on a prior distinction between aesthetically noteworthy and aesthetically unnoteworthy qualities. Thus, to decide which qualities are aesthetically noteworthy, we cannot first decide which ones are exemplified; we must work in the opposite direction, since we do not know what is exemplified until we know what is noteworthy. It follows that in deciding how good a music-work is, from the aesthetic point of view—in judging, for example, that opus 101 is a great sonata—we need not take into account the exemplificational aspect of the work. We do need to take into account its noteworthy qualities, both merits and defects, and these will be, as a matter of fact, the exemplified ones, on the principle proposed. But what makes them count in critical judgments is logically prior to, and independent of, their exemplificationality. Hence, though the critic need not deny this aspect of music, he is not invited to dwell on it or pursue its ramifications, but rather is enjoined to turn his full attention to the qualities themselves, as they are heard in the work, and to the structures they both hang on to and help to hold together.

On the modest or restrained theory of musical reference defended here, it is pre- cisely properties—not objects or events or processes or emotional states that occur in or belong to the extramusical world—that are referred to. In this respect the theory differs importantly from those of the other four thinkers we have considered and, indeed, from nearly all thinkers who have defended theories of musical "meaning." But we are all convinced that there is *some* connection between music and the world. On the exemplification theory it is just this: many of the qualities of music-works are shared with other things. Sad music sounds the way sadness feels: that was Carroll C. Pratt's formula, and it remains a true and telling one, I think. It implies no reference from the music to the emotion, but it reports a common quality, and an interesting one. This is not true of all musical qualities, of course: many are to be found, in their specific flavor, nowhere else, and they are no less valuable from the aesthetic point of view. But similarities have a special importance.

Such similarities, for example, underlie and sustain our metaphorical descriptions of music in terms derived from wider ranges of our experience: the passage rushes headlong or it is in travail, it is bitter or meditative. We are apt to recognize these most important qualities which come and go through a music-work, which enable it to insinuate itself in our activities or assimilate itself to verbal programs, song lyrics, and the movements of a dance. But the more important shared properties of music are much less often noted, and by way of conclusion I shall say just a little about them.

The kind of property I have in mind is brought out very well in a fine study of Beethoven's opus 101 by the Australian musicologist, Kay Dreyfus. She begins a summary of her conclusions by remarking: "In this sonata, then, it is the Finale that provides the clue as to what kind of musical statement the work has presented. It is not a statement that is concerned with the conflict or confrontation of opposing ideas. . . . What the work *is* concerned with is the gradual discovery and unleashing of a capacity for growth and sustained development within the material introduced by the opening idea of the first movement."[43] If the word "statement" in the first sentence seemed to suggest that an informative message was about to be read off the musical text, the switch to "concern" should correct the misapprehension. The term "statement" is one of Dreyfus's technical terms, and is quite innocuous in context (though in general I favor avoiding terms that *can* be misleading in this way). She is describing the emergence and unleashing of the capacity for (musical) growth that occurs in the course of this sonata. Her theory of opus 101, her proposed configurational understanding of its fundamental character, is that it moves from extraordinary constriction and constraint in the first movement to great assertiveness and breadth of activity in the finale. "In the first movement itself, attempts at the extension and development of the phrases were seen to be equally ineffectual, and a technique of delayed resolution—of the perpetual avoidance of the anticipated cadential close —was substituted for development. Two important features of the musical situation presented in the first movement were its tonal inconclusiveness (seen in the avoidance of a strong articulation of the tonic key and in the high degree of incidental chromaticism) and its extreme brevity."[44] When she speaks of "ineffectual" attempts at development, she does not, of course, mean Beethoven's attempts, but rather the attempts of the phrases themselves (metaphorically speaking) to develop into larger patterns, realizing their potentialities for growth or, failing that, to find resolution and closure. It is Beethoven who artfully frustrates these phrases, to make way for the first break-out in the march that follows.

So we have a striking form of growth enacted, presented in concentrated form, displayed. The work is not like the maple tree by your window, growing (I trust) at its own deliberate pace, offering an occasion for reflection on growth in general, if you are so inclined, but not especially inviting—much less insisting upon—such abstract thought. It is more like a motion picture made up of frames exposed at weekly intervals, so that in a few seconds you see the tree raise up and unfold its branches. Here growth is loud and clear; it is what the film features. So, too, with opus 101 on Dreyfus's understanding of it. Although it does not, like the film, represent anything else, so much happens so vividly, in a mere nineteen and one-half minutes, between the first notes and the last, in the way of musical growth, that the sonata can be said to show its "concern" with growth in general, to exemplify that property.

And growth is a very fundamental kind of change, characterizing our life-experience when it is most successful and most rewarding, though hampered, as it may be, by obstacles to be overcome. Music is change, and in a sense it is nothing more than change in its myriad forms and ways, and in this respect it is a mirror or match for some of the most fundamental features of our personal lives and social histories. There is, I believe, profound insight in some words written by Leonard Meyer in his review of Donald Ferguson's book: "In other words, music is a metaphor not primarily because, as Ferguson contends, it depicts the feelings and ideas connected with particular events in the extra-musical world, but because music is a model, an archetype, of all experience—experience in which making inferences and predictions, sensing ambiguities, feeling uncertainties, and revising opinions are the most basic facts there are in a world of probability."[45] I am not reconciled to this extended use of the term "metaphor," which seems, like some of the other words here, to concede the (unwarranted) claim that music "depicts" feelings and ideas. And the word "model" must be understood with care. But the idea that music exemplifies—indeed, exploits and glories in—aspects of change that are among the most fundamental and pervasive characteristics of living seems to me true. Music, we might say, is in essence *continuation*: the question is always where it will take us next, and every happening is marked by the sense that possibilities are opening or closing, that there is development or retrogression, that there is continuity or abruptness, doubt or decisiveness, hesitancy or determination, building or disintegration.[46]

Because these patterns or modes of continuation are such general features of all experience, I may be forgiven for yielding to the temptation to call them "metaphysical"—thus, in a way placing myself in the company of Schopenhauer, whose insight into such matters I very much respect, although I cannot subscribe to his own metaphysics. I do not say, remember, that in composing or performing music one is *attributing* these modes of continuation to human experience or to the worlds of nature and history, or even that one is *referring* to these realities. But if our inquiry has led to a true conclusion, built on Nelson Goodman's important concept, then the modes of continuation themselves *are* referred to by the music, and what makes them metaphysical is just that they are shared by so much besides music. Hence, among other points to be briefly noted in a moment, the natural, the intense, the perennial interest they must have for us, touching in this way on our personal and social destinies.

I do not wish to be committed for present purposes, to the view that all music is essentially characterized by Edmund Gurney's "ideal motion" in a strict sense— though I am tempted on other occasions to insist on this, even in the face of a wide-spread compositional practice that seems, at least, to run counter to such a claim. How often do we read criticism of new music that runs like the following comment on Charlie Morrow's *Wave Music III*, for sixty clarinets, whose players are mostly moving about as they perform? "Various thematic permutations [on a "basic four-note motif"], along with some improvising that was theoretically limited to certain players but seemed to spread in epidemic fashion, kept the essentially static music from becoming repetitive."[47] I am not alluding to the commonly made (and charitable) suggestion that the merit of a new work consists in narrowly avoiding acute boredom, but rather to the phrase "essentially static music." Even in avant-garde works that do not move, or hardly move at all in the sense in which a melody or tonal chord progression does, there is still *continuation*—something (or nothing) has to happen next, if only another sound or prolongation of the same sound. Lack of change is also a manner or mode of continuation. That something remains constant (for some time) is a fundamental and pervasive character of our experience, too. However, I do not mean to concede that sounding a single note for ten minutes will exemplify a very interesting form of persistence through time, in comparison, say, to a passacaglia theme that remains invariant through its variations.

It would be interesting, I think, to consider aleatoric music from this point of view (though I will make only a few brief remarks here). By "aleatoric music" I mean music in which the succession of musical events is produced, not by deliberate intention, but by chance. Such a procedure has been given various justifications. For example, some critics say that no continuation is preferable to any other. But this is not true, since some continuations display metaphysical qualities that others do not, or not so clearly or vividly—and this is a ground of preference. The fallacy is understandable. In a sense, every continuation does provide an *instance* of some *kind* of continuation; but we have seen that displaying is more than being a mere instance —just as it is not every strawberry that can be used to exemplify the characteristic or ideal qualities of the strawberry. Another justification of aleatoric music is that if you are patient, then, just by chance, something interesting may happen. And if you have got plenty of time and sixty clarinets to play around with, perhaps the odds on your side are enough to tempt a gambler. Sometimes the aleatoric composer does indeed get continuations that no one might have thought of or (consequently) have intended, and yet are metaphysically exemplary. But in the short term this is not likely, and audiences must be forgiven if they wander away in search of better odds.

The metaphysical modes of continuation that are deeply apprehended in music must account for much of its capacity to move us. I am not sure I can go along with all of Leonard Meyer's claim that "musical suspense seems to have direct analogies in experience in general; it makes us feel something of the insignificance and powerlessness of man in the face of the inscrutable workings of destiny."[48] But suspense is disturbing in whatever form it assumes, and the release from it correspondingly heartening and gladdening. So, too, disintegration is threatening, reversal astonishing, loss of power and drive unsettling, delayed fulfillment anxiety-producing, missed opportunity poignant; but growth is encouraging, revival inspiriting, arrival satisfying. Triumph over obstacles arouses confidence, and endurance, respect. As they occur in music, these modes of continuation have a fictive character, since nothing is really happening to us; but they nevertheless have power to affect us.[49] Moreover, in this metaphysical view of music, it is not surprising that we can be moved again and again by the same music-work, that the things that happen in it, the special forms of continuation it exhibits, can be momentous and full of significance even when we know them by heart.

Finally—and rather speculatively—music may have the power to instruct us as well, in a certain sense. Here I am agreeing with Nelson Goodman once more, for his emphasis has been steadily on the cognitive aspects of aesthetic encounter.[50] Much remains to be clarified and explained on this point, so I risk only a few rather vague remarks, just to make sure that this possibility does not get lost sight of. The music-work does not need to refer to anything else besides its own aesthetically notable qualities in order to play its role in helping us to understand our world and cope with it. Here is where the infinite subtlety, variety, and plasticity of music come into play. Music can make extremely delicate distinctions between kinds of continuation, between two slightly different forms of ambiguity or of headlong rushing or of growth. It thereby can sharpen our apprehension of such differences, and give us concepts of continuation that we might miss in ordinary experience, under the press of affairs, but yet that we can bring to experience (as "models," perhaps) with fresh perceptiveness and clearer cognitive grasp. I think there is some truth in this.

Notes

1. See Joseph Kerman, "The State of Academic Music Criticism," Chapter 3 in this volume.
2. Ibid.
3. Ibid.
4. For example, first movement, bars 135-43; second movement, bars 60-67; fourth movement, bars 55-65, 181-91.
5. Frantisek Bartos, *Bedrich Smetana: Letters and Reminiscences,* trans. Daphne Rusbridge (Prague: Artia, 1955), p. 189-91, letter from Smetana in Jabkenice to Josef Srb-Debrnov.
6. Richard Kuhns, "Music as a Representational Art," *British Journal of Aesthetics* 18 (1978): 123.
7. *New York Times,* 20 June, 1971.
8. Tamara Grum-Grzhimailo, "Glimpses of Shostakovich," *Soviet Life* (December 1971), no. 183, p. 39.
9. David Epstein, *Beyond Orpheus: Studies in Musical Structure* (Cambridge, Mass.: MIT Press, 1979), p. 203.
10. Benjamin Boretz, "Nelson Goodman's *Languages of Art* from a Musical Point of View," *Journal of Philosophy* 67 (1970): 548.
11. Karl Aschenbrenner, *The Concepts of Criticism* (Boston: Reidel, Dordrecht, 1974), Part II. I have discussed the book critically in a review: *Journal of Aesthetics and Art Criticism* 34 (Winter 1975): 199-202.
12. See "Music Criticism: Practice and Malpractice," Chapter 6 in this volume.
13. Ibid.
14. Ibid.
15. See Rose Rosengard Subotnik, "Romantic Music as Post-Kantian Critique," chapter 5 in this volume.
16. Ibid.
17. Deryck Cooke, *The Language of Music* (New York: Oxford University Press, 1959), p. 25.
18. Ibid., p. xii.
19. Ibid., p. 14.
20. Ibid., p. 64.
21. Ibid., pp. 231-32.
22. Donald M. Ferguson, *Music as Metaphor: The Elements of Expression* (Minneapolis: University of Minnesota Press, 1960), p. vii; cf. p. 72.
23. Ibid., p. 14.
24. Ibid., p. 52.
25. Ibid., pp. 64-79, 87.
26. Ibid., p. 162.
27. Gordon Epperson, *The Musical Symbol: A Study of the Philosophic Theory of Music* (Ames: Iowa State University Press, 1967), pp. 9-10.
28. Ibid., p. 169.

29. Wilson Coker, *Music and Meaning: A Theoretical Introduction to Musical Aesthetics* (New York: The Free Press, 1970), pp. 154-58.

30. Ibid., p. 30.

31. Ibid., p. 18.

32. Ibid., p. 155.

33. Ibid., p. 168.

34. Ibid., pp. 2-3.

35. Ibid., p. 2.

36. On musical quotation, see Nelson Goodman, "On Some Questions Concerning Quotation," *Monist* 58 (1974): 294-306; and Vernon A. Howard, "On Musical Quotation," *Monist* 58 (1974): 307-18.

37. See Charles Rosen, "Influence: Plagiarism and Inspiration," Chapter 2 in this volume.

38. Ibid.

39. Ibid.

40. Nelson Goodman, *Languages of Art: An Approach to a Theory of Symbols* (Indianapolis: Hackett Publishing Co., 1976).

41. See Monroe C. Beardsley, "Semiotic Aesthetics and Aesthetic Education," *Journal of Aesthetic Education* 9 (1975): 5-26, and "*Languages of Art* and Art Criticism," *Erkenntnis* 12 (1978): 95-118, also pp. 169-73.

42. See Geoffrey Payzant, *Glenn Gould, Music and Mind* (Toronto: Van Nostrand Reinhold, 1978), esp. pp. 57-62.

43. "Beethoven's Last Five Piano Sonatas" (Ph.D. diss., University of Melbourne, 1971), p. 74.

44. Ibid.

45. Leonard Mayer, *Journal of American Musicological Society* 15 (1962): 236.

46. These ideas have affinities with some interesting work on "temporal process" being done by David B. Greene, as in his paper at a session of the American Society of Value Inquiry, Boston, December 1976 and in other essays (forthcoming).

47. Robert Palmer, in *New York Times*, 23 June, 1979.

48. Leonard Meyer, *Emotion and Meaning in Music* (Chicago: University of Chicago Press, 1956), p. 28.

49. Moreover, I would say that some poems move us at a level of abstraction approaching that of the metaphysical qualities of music; a meditation on mutability in general, or on the inexorable passage of time, or on the steadfastness of loyalty or love.

50. Indeed, as Nelson Goodman has pointed out to me, what I have been saying comports with passages in his *Ways of Worldmaking* (Indianapolis: Hackett Publishing Co., 1978), pp. 105-6.

5

Romantic Music
as Post-Kantian Critique:
Classicism, Romanticism, and the
Concept of the Semiotic Universe

ROSE ROSENGARD SUBOTNIK

IN THE ATTEMPT to develop a critical language capable of characterizing musical classicism adequately, a useful starting point is provided by the notion that in certain respects this style suggests as its structural model a cognitive system—logic, assuming logic is defined broadly. For both the characteristic classical structure (which could be referred to loosely as a sonata structure) and the logical demonstration seem to propose the same ideal of the semiotic structure as a semiotic universe, a universe that can be described succinctly as an autonomous intelligible whole.[1] Just as a logical argument contains its own premises and conclusions, which define themselves in temporal succession, so, too, the characteristic classical structure seems to include a temporally unifying tonal premise out of which it is possible to imagine that the entire structure, in all its parameters, is rationally derived. As a result, the classical musical structure seems capable, at least in its normative state, of embodying all of its meaning within its own, internally determined structural boundaries. Thus its structure suggests itself as a semiotic whole.

The characteristic classical movement, moreover, seems to manifest a structure of tonally based premise and conclusion at each of many hierarchical levels, from its encompassing plan down to the pairings of antecedent-consequent phrases that constitute its typical structural unit. And in classical music, as in logic, the temporally defined connections between premise and conclusion appear to be necessary. There is, indeed, a degree to which, like the language used in a logical demonstration, the

I wish to thank here the American Council of Learned Societies and the Guggenheim Foundation for the fellowships that made possible the development of this piece.

"art" in a mature symphony by Haydn in particular suggests itself as a kind of window onto a syntactically true structure, an underlying structure that is necessary, and hence true, in itself. And since classical music, unlike baroque, lacks all semblance of the external object or *signifié* characteristic in cognitive discourse, it would appear to be even more self-contained, more purely syntactic than logic, and thus closer to truth, by standards of logic, than is logic itself.[2]

It could be said, of course, that all cognitive structures, even logic, by virtue of their cognitive character seem ultimately to make some sort of direct claim about the reality of the world outside of their own language, if only the claim that the relationships they describe actually exist.[3] By comparison, classical music, in the seeming totality of its truth of coherence, appears to forfeit all claim to any direct truth of correspondence. Still, within the bounds of its own structure, classical music seems to affirm as valid that pattern of cognitively necessary connections between the complementary sorts of structures—structures such as antecedent-consequent, cause and effect, and even subject and object—through which cognitive thought ordinarily seems to promise a verifiable connection between man's conceptual structures and the external world. Just as, in Kantian terms, the unity of logic can encompass a manifold of sensory data, so, too, by implying within the particularity of its structure the entire hierarchy of systematic tonal relationships, the classical structure seems able to encompass within its own rational framework the diversity of a whole universe.

Classical music, moreover, seems to project itself, at some level, as Everyman's art, an art that Everyman can imagine himself creating as he hears it unfolding in time, paradoxically, because this music, in exposing its own premises, suggests that it can be generally verified as meeting exacting and exclusionary standards, the standards of rightness and wrongness. In other words, the style that has been taken for the very norm of musical art seems to have accepted as its own normative standard of judgment a criterion ordinarily associated with the objectivity or apparent autonomy of cognitive structures, the capacity to embody truth. But of course, the classical structure can convey the impression of embodying universally verifiable truth only because its own structure is somehow imaginable as universally comprehensible, as a universe of discourse encompassing all men as "competent" interpreters. Beyond an innate human capacity to understand the self-evident necessity of its internal structural connections as they are unfolded over time, it seems to promise that nothing is needed to understand it—no outside information, no specialized cultural knowledge, training, or ideally, even identity. Its seemingly pure intrastructural meaning projects itself as open to all who have the musical equivalent of a faculty of reason.

If, however, one points to logic as a structural archetype for the classical style, then it is important to note the qualifications that are necessitated in ordinary conceptions of logic by Kant's critical philosophy, a philosophy precisely contemporary with the maturity of Haydn and Mozart.[4] Thus, though a logical structure is indeed a syntactic structure, it cannot, Kant makes clear, be considered an *absolutely*

autonomous intelligible structure, a structure necessary or true in itself, for to be so it would have to exist in some metaphysical realm of being beyond intelligibility as man understands that term. Instead, the structure of a logical demonstration must be viewed simply as the analogical projection of an entire structure existing somewhere within a human mind. In other words, inasmuch as a logical demonstration is a semiotic structure rather than a structure beyond the possibility of meaning, its "autonomy" must be defined as a paradoxical state of physical discreteness and fixity which is yet formally dependent on a subjective mind that designates its internal connections as necessary or true, and imbues it with meaning.

Furthermore, Kant clarifies that no cognitive structure, including logic, can make a cognitively certain connection between the internal mental structure on which it depends and any realm wholly external to the mind. For insofar as they can be known, all of the complementary pairs encompassed within cognition, including subject and object, amount to structures that take their form from some internal subjective structure and thus are not, in that form, to be taken as elements of two distinct realms of being. Indeed, from the account given in Kant's *Critique of Judgment*, one can conclude that what seem to be complementary constructs bound in pairs through cognition are actually more like analogues themselves, related to each other only in the parallel or disjunct sense in which analogues can be related. At any rate, though cognitive semiotic structures, through a discreteness of *signifiant* and *signifié*, point explicitly toward two discrete levels of being, even they can be construed, finally, as no more than one-dimensional or entirely syntactic systems; the most nearly certain knowledge they can be assumed to convey is a knowledge by analogy of the mental structures that project them.

Thus, logical knowledge has no absolute objectivity, but is bound by the limits of a subjective structure. However, even within the limits of its subjective realm, cognition, no matter how far extended, cannot, solely through its own rules of theoretical reason, define a rationally whole system or universe.[5] For sooner or later, cognition encounters contradictions or irrationalities that it cannot resolve. True, the mind can, according to Kant, imagine such a resolution to occur at a level of mental being inaccessible to knowledge, and the *Critique of Judgment* suggests how the other two mental faculties, judgment and practical reason, can account for what seems irrationality to cognition. But the structures of these other faculties cannot ultimately be synthesized in any wholly rational way with that of cognition; they can only draw the same data into their own domains. Hence, the realm of cognition itself, which includes logic, can never be counted as a knowable rational whole.

This inability to know the realm of cognition as a rational whole, moreover, has a corollary, which assumes prominence with Kant, in man's inability to know any particular, empirically defined cognitive structure in its entirety. For though man's cognitive structures, for example, his logical demonstrations, are to be understood as analogues of whole inner mental structures, man does not know with certainty the ultimate basis of either his outer or his inner cognitive structures, which he does not, after all, form consciously. Indeed, despite Kant's derivation of apparently pure (that is, nonempirical or formal) and, therefore, ultimate cognitive structures—the famous categories of the *Critique of Pure Reason*—from empirically used linguistic constructions, his account actually invites the conclusion that one can neither know with certainty the composition (which would, of course, include the intrinsic rationality) of any ultimate mental structure nor certify the ultimacy of any mental structure that is projected as ultimate. This is precisely because such structures are conceded by Kant to exist not simply within the mind of the individual, at a level accessible to complete rational verification, but rather behind or beneath the mind, at a so-called transcendental level of abstraction, beyond the reach of either logical or empirical proof, a level where they can only be imagined as plausible, or at most posited, in axiomatic fashion, as ultimate archetypes of empirically known cognitive structures. In other words, Kant's desire to preserve a universal basis for cognition forces him to locate that basis at a level of nonempirical formality, where it becomes inaccessible to human cognition, which, as he stresses throughout the *Critique of Judgment*, operates exclusively in conjunction with the senses, that is, by way of either sense-data or empirically defined symbols (such as words or geometric shapes).

To be sure, in locating the fundamental structures of the mind at a level beyond the reach of all conscious control, experience, and subjective or cultural variance —and it is extremely significant that Kant does not recognize concrete cultural limits on the "purely formal" cognitive categories he derives from culturally particular (Western) linguistic structures—Kant not only finds a workable way of designating such structures as universal, and as such rational, but also locates them at a level that is as resistant to conclusive disproof as it is to conclusive proof. It is in this sense that although he can no longer ground the universality of cognitive truth, including logical truth, with cognitive certainty in any absolute objective or metaphysical level of being, Kant can claim to have preserved at least the formal possibility of such truth on purely subjective grounds, the grounds of human mental structure.

Nevertheless, it must be emphasized that grounding subjective universality at a transcendental level of thought or being by definition precludes establishing that universality as a cognitive certainty and exposes the fact, in a sense recognized but never fully analyzed by Kant, that ultimately it is no more possible to prove connections between structures existing within two separate minds than it is to prove connections between subjective and extrasubjective levels of being. At most, within the terms of Kant's critical philosophy, if one leaves out the moral desirability of such connections, one can posit only the formal possibility of analogies between subjective structures.

To put it more simply, once man has accepted the terms of the critical philosophy and reduced the field of human knowledge to the structure of the forms through which his own mind works, then no device, not even the device of transendental subjectivity, can spare him from admitting that the only mental structures he himself knows anything about and can deal with cognitively, at a level beyond merely naming them as formal possibilities, are concrete, particularized, or "mediated" structures. Even within his own mind, any abstract structure for which man may look (if it exists at all) has already been mediated, at least through the concreteness of sensory images and generally through some physically and culturally particular system of language as well. One can posit the blind fact, so to speak, of an abstract analogue to these concrete structures: one can posit an archetypal structure that is at once similar to known structures and yet not identical. But one cannot know for certain the existence, rationality, or exact form of such an archetype.

Is it then possible to have such knowledge with respect to other men's minds or to deduce with certainty a universal archetype from the external semiotic structures through which man signifies and communicates? Since no mental structure can know or control entirely its appearance from the outside, it must undergo substantial mediation to externalize itself, and the resultant externalized structure must be still further mediated for interpretation by others. Hence, although it is often useful to posit such a universal structure, and even though, if Kant is right, one seems more or less forced by the rules of (Western) reason to do so, at least in certain contexts, nevertheless one has no cognitively certain basis for describing such a structure, for assigning its existence anything more than a heuristic status, or for defining its presence in any semiotic structure, or process, as more than a formal possibility.[6]

In fact, the adoption of Kant's critical attitude leads to a consciousness of the irreducible differences between all known and conceivable semiotic structures. It brings about awareness that, precisely by virtue of the physical and cultural definition that allows even the semblance of communication, all externalized semiotic structures must be assumed to distort any internal structure, whether abstract or concrete, that may have projected them. And to the extent that the physical (and even cultural) domains of being are beyond conscious, subjective, or rational control, external semiotic structures must also be assumed to incorporate elements of arbitrariness (such as Saussure's signs) which elude demonstrable rules for usage and open up these semiotic structures to misunderstanding, and which invariably place an empirical restriction on the number of those competent in each system. Thus, just as the only individual mind to which man can claim access is an empirically particular mind—broader in the sense of being more concrete, yet narrower in range than any transcendental mental structure—so, too, the broadest subjective structure to which man can claim access must be imagined to have an empirically real or "mediated" existence and therefore to be cultural rather than universal. Even the cultural structure has no clear status of cognitive certainty.[7]

Consequently, a full acceptance of Kant's epistemological position requires renunciation of any cognitively certain basis for regarding communication as a direct and accurate connection between subjective structures. At most, the post-Kantian is justified in thinking of semiotic processes as indirect, consisting in the establishment of a series of structures, both internal mental ones and external or autonomous ones, as analogous. In terms of such a process, an autonomous semiotic structure can be characterized as whole only in the sense of having a more or less discrete and fixed physical existence, accessible as such to perception by one or more subjective minds. It cannot be assumed to be a whole in the sense that it is rationally knowable in all of its potential meaning by any individual; for without an established universality of structure among its potential interpreters, the autonomous semiotic structure cannot be construed as having any intrinsic meaning at all. One can imagine it to have only that meaning that is imposed upon it by subjective minds, no two of which need perceive it in the same way even if each mind perceives it as its own structural analogue.[8] For a post-Kantian, the communication of any particular meaning must be accepted as a contingent process.

From what has been said already about the classical style in music, it should be clear that here, too, one could characterize certain structural elements as pointing toward a universalized and quasi-objective conception of subjectivity similar to Kant's transcendental subjective structure. Most suggestive in this respect, no doubt, is the tonal principle that today is generally associated with the term "sonata." On the one hand, it seems to underlie the temporal structure of most movements by Haydn, Mozart, and Beethoven (at least up until his later works, and possibly even then). On the other hand, theorists reiterate that the sonata-allegro, or whatever they choose to call it, exists as an abstraction only; it is, to use Charles Rosen's words, a "unifying principle" rather than a "preexistent shape."[9] Again, the quasi-logical way in which the classical composer draws upon the structural implications of tonality allows him by and large to suggest an avoidance of that arbitrariness which is apparently inseparable from the concrete mediation of abstract structures. In Beethoven's music, where the binding force of tonality is first explicitly exposed to question, the presence of stylistic particularity and, hence, of potential grounds for a general effect of arbitrariness can no longer be overlooked, even in an idealized characterization such as this. With Mozart and especially Haydn, however, it is often possible to entertain the illusion that the empirical particularity and arbitrariness of style have been integrated seamlessly with the universal necessity of an abstract musical structure, so that one could momentarily believe that the style *is* the structure and that for this music, stylistic understanding (the stylistic perception or, in a sense, the apprehension of structure as a surface) and structural understanding (the understanding of structural meaning or the apprehension of internal structural connections) are identical.

With classical music, however, as with logical discourse, the semiotic process can be established only as a contingent delineation of analogies, not as that effecting of necessary connections which would follow from the demonstrable existence of a universal subjective structure. Thus, none of the syntactic connections effected within classical music or, hence, the meanings that can be attached to those connections, can be considered necessary in itself at either the most narrowly technical or the most broadly philosophical levels of interpretation. Thus, the movement from the tonic to the dominant key in a major-mode classical movement is "inevitable" only in the sense that, as Rosen points out, "it was a necessary condition of intelligibility" for the audience of its time and place.[10] Furthermore, even if it were generally agreed that by basing its entire structure on normative principles, such as the need to resolve implications properly, classical music designated implicit universal intelligibility as the normative ideal of art, it would not follow that such intelligibility necessarily is the proper goal of art. Instead, one could posit this norm of classical music as the mediated analogue or variant of some underlying structure that could at best be identified, and from the outside only, as a particular structure.

We would most likely call that particular structure in this case a value of Enlightenment culture. Other sorts of syntactic connections, such as reference to the opening thematic material at some point in the second part of a sonata exposition or an infusion of chromatic harmony into the diatonic context of a sonata movement, we would attribute, rather, to some archetypal structure within the mind of a particular individual, here Haydn and Mozart, respectively.[11] Mozart's music, indeed, presents such a palpably sensuous surface that in any account less generalized than this, one would have to investigate the ways in which the particularity of his style diverges from the logic of his structure and, thus, the extent to which his music deviates from its own classical norms. In fact, we would eventually have to conclude from a genuinely critical analysis of any classical music that to make sense of the pattern of syntactic connections within a semiotic structure, no matter how forcefully that structure suggested itself as meaningful and thereby evoked the idea of an autonomous or implicit meaning, it was necessary to assume some analogical conformity between that pattern and some particular subjective conception underlying it of the needs of structure. Such a conception we associate, by and large, with the notion of style, either individual or cultural; it is a conception that we can "know" only through the mediation of our own particular mental structures.

As one final sort of evidence for the notion that classical music as a semiotic structure actually works by way of contingent analogy rather than necessary connections, it could be noted that classical music in fact falls considerably short of achieving implicit universal intelligibility. True, the style succeeds for many educated listeners in projecting the norm of a semiotic autonomy in which a more or less logical universality of structure wholly absorbs particularity of style. In actuality, however, classical music probably comes closer to defining something like that Enlightenment ideal of Everyman described by Jacques Barzun as "a clothed creature, whose proper, because logical, language is French, and whose destiny is to live according to the Christian religion under an hereditary king."[12] Like most manifestations of the universalistic ideals of the Enlightenment, which turn out to be normative in an exclusionary sense, classical musical structure has in fact been found understandable by only a relatively small number of people, even within Western society, people for whom, we can suppose, that musical structure constitutes some recognizable variant of an internal conception of meaningful structure. For the rest of society it would appear that the particularity of style in the classical work, be it cultural or individual particularity, obscures the clarity of structure.

Enlightenment rationalists, including Kant himself, looked down on music for the weakness of its capacity to signify cognitively.[13] In fact, "pure" music seems to expose the limitations of all man's semiotic structures in a somewhat paradigmatic fashion. This exposure becomes more dramatically clear in romantic music, as will be seen, but even classical music, with all its quasi-logical clarity, suggests finally that the meaning of all semiotic structures, even that of logic, can be verified only through an explicitly intrasubjective or one-dimensional establishment of a state of analogy, a state that is indemonstrable, contingent, and internally disjunct. This is a state that Kant himself associates specifically with aesthetic judgment, wherein sensory perception or imagination and abstract or conceptual understanding are defined essentially as disjunct, equally subjective faculties that are at most related through the contingent state of analogy, and wherein a proper object, typically a beautiful structure,[14] establishes such a state of analogy, thereby defining itself in essence as structurally analogous to judgment.[15] Indeed, in suggesting logic as its own structural model, classical music, which has been taken for the norm of musical art, seems to do precisely what Kant's critical philosophy appears to do in spite of itself: reveal the necessity of logic as nothing more than an aesthetic necessity.

As logic, with its self-embodied truth and necessary connections, loses status as a model of universal truth in the wake of the critical philosophy, one might expect to find an increasing emphasis in music on properties of the analogy, the pattern that Kant in effect links with his reduced concept of the truth accessible to man. In fact, such properties do become evident at many levels of nineteenth-century music. Indeed, romantic music seems to take up Kant's critical principle in some analogous fashion of its own and use it explicitly to undermine the classical ideal of the semiotic universe. In the nineteenth century, the classical norm of an autonomous universe encompassing all of its own meaning seems to have been shattered into a new cultural paradigm of many semiotic universes, universes that are separated by irreducible differences of total identity and are yet analogous in their emphasis on particularity. And just as the notion of a particular universe (like that of subjective "autonomy") is paradoxical, so, too, the paradigmatic nineteenth-century semiotic structure, at least in music, seems, by virtue of its particularity, to be markedly autonomous as pure, externally defined, physical structure, and yet, explicitly incomplete in meaning. As a result, whereas the classical musical structure projects the illusion of involving a logical sort of competence, one that permits the establishment of necessary connections between disparate minds or their externalized structures, the romantic musical structure seems openly to acknowledge that it can count only on modes of competence that involve the contingency of analogy. Rather than assuming or evoking "universal" normative notions of right and wrong, romantic music seems simply to want and to seek an understanding of what it is saying, and thereby to acknowledge the very act of understanding as problematical.[16]

Thus, for example, music of the nineteenth century tends to renounce a normative conception of structure in the sense that tonality stops patterning itself on the logical model of premise-and-conclusion and ceases to resemble a universal norm. The functional use of harmonies for purposes audibly explainable in terms of large-scale temporal structure gives way increasingly to structurally arbitrary "coloristic" uses of harmony, highly varied for individualized purposes; established rules for the choice of scale degrees and chord progressions are at times broken so as to admit effects of modality, which are not merely subversive in effect, like chromaticism, but openly irreconcilable with tonal relationships; and tonality in general loses its effect of determining whole structures and governing the other musical parameters.

Once tonality ceases to function as a universal norm, however, music clearly loses its capacity to project itself as a semiotically autonomous structure, a structure embodying all of its meaning in its internal connections. Indeed, centrally involved in this loss is an apparent disintegration of those connections or, more generally, of the structural cohesiveness out of which the classical musical component seems to have derived its meaning. For, characteristically in romantic music, the temporally unified wholeness of tonal argument gives way to a pervasive individuation, which tends at every level of the musical structure to define semiotic units that cannot be rejoined in any imminent structural sense because, though incomplete as a source of meaning, they are also, in a physical sense, self-contained or autonomous.

Only a few examples of this tendency can be suggested here. Typically, in romantic music, the purely implicative propulsiveness of tonality tends to work in audible fashion on the more "localized" levels of the passage or segment (which, to be sure, can be sizeable in literal terms), rather than at the overarching level of the whole piece. Similarly, there is a tendency to strip the antecedent-consequent phrase of its implicitly large-scale structural significance by dissociating it from the function of a tonal premise and reducing it to one of many harmonic (or even primarily melodic) components too self-contained to imply, so that even when an entire structure is dominated by the recurrence of the antecedent-consequent pattern, the pattern has only a localized effect. Corollary temporal signs of this disintegration, all with clear precedents in Beethoven's music, include an increase in the static repetition or variance of self-contained units (which are defined as discrete in identity rather than joined through development); the building up of thematic patterns or rhythmic momentum through a cumulative repetition or variance of discrete units;[17] abrupt and harmonically unprepared shifts of tonal plane; and close juxtaposition of major and minor modes, especially of major and minor forms of the same chord (a technique that not only produces harmonic ambiguity, but also emphasizes harmonic identity as an individual element over the long-range constructive powers of functional harmonic implication).[18] All of these devices tend to vitiate the effect of an intelligible, temporally defined wholeness in romantic music by undercutting both overall cohesiveness and also the internally effected determinacy of the outer boundaries of a structure. And all, it should be noted, constitute striking evidence for the notion that romantic music, here at the level of temporal structure, takes on manifest characteristics of a field of individual analogues, not only in terms of the physical appearance it offers to perception but also in terms of the possibilities it allows for interpretation. For in order to derive a cohesive meaning from such elements of temporal structure, a meaning in relation to a whole, one is openly forced to impose from without connections between them of one's own making, that is, to construct a kind of individualized interpretative or critical structure that is in some sense an analogue to the structure externalized by the composer.

If structure in romantic music, as in classical music, is defined narrowly, as an abstract internal relationality or as the temporal and quasi-logical or, essentially, tonal unfolding of events, then most romantic works lack a complete internal structural intelligibility and present themselves, regardless of size, as semiotic fragments rather than universes. (Paradoxically, therefore, those that seem the least incomplete are often literally very small.) This means that the meaning and even the rationality of most actual romantic structures, when set against this narrow, temporal definition of structure, become clearly open to question, even when use is made of traditional or easily stereotyped structures, since such forms tend to seem imposed, like preexistent blocks, upon the harmonic material of the romantic piece rather than to project themselves as evolving temporally out of some internally defined necessity. One loses the sense in romantic music that a piece employing such a form can be analyzed logically from within as its temporal connections unfold. Instead, it becomes necessary to wait until the piece is complete and one is outside of it, able consciously to perceive or construe it as a fixed object, in order to analyze it, and then only on the empirical basis of what actually happened in it — a process that is clearly arbitrary since no general rules for structural analysis can be deduced from the mere existence of successive events that are governed by no implicit connective principle.

Consequently, whereas classical structure seems to promise its own explanation, the intrinsic character of romantic temporal structure is such that in order to understand its rationale one must acquire techniques of retrospective analysis. And since the harmonic elements of romantic structure no longer seem to carry out a self-evident logical argument (and are often highly complex), specialized training in romantic practice is manifestly required before one can attempt to explain the significance of those elements on both the large scale and the small, thereby gaining some idea of the kinds of significance that might be involved. Thus, in shifting from a normative ideal of competence, such as the ability to judge correctness, romantic music actually increases the difficulty of understanding its individual temporal structure. Unlike competence in logic (or in natural language, as it is ordinarily used), structural competence in romantic music seems to require a self-conscious perception of an entire structure; unlike its counterpart in classical music, structural competence in romantic music openly demands specialized empirical knowledge and training.[19] Of course, although this training can be acquired, it need not be. Given the difficulties involved in obtaining it, romantic expertise is apt to be limited to a small number of specialists who may, in fact, have trouble communicating any understanding of structural connections that goes beyond an ability merely to perceive or describe individual elements. Even these specialists generally have no clear basis for knowing that the semiotic connections they impose on the romantic musical structure are "right," since the individuality of romantic harmonic practice and temporal conceptions tends explicitly to preclude general norms of correctness with respect to the internal connections of a musical structure. On the whole, it would seem that musical specialists can at most claim authority to pronounce romantic works not "right," but "elegant" or "good," since, as Kant makes clear in the *Critique of Judgment*, grounds for the latter sort of judgment are without question indemonstrable.

In brief, the patent lack of semiotic wholeness and the individualized, empirical character of the romantic temporal or harmonic structure tend to emphasize the contingent and specialized status of structural competence in this music. This emphasis precludes any identification of the structurally competent with the general listener, so that if competence in romantic music, as in classical music, is defined as structural competence, that is, as competence with respect to temporal connectedness, then the probability is strong that no listener is totally competent and that most listeners are incompetent.[20] Unlike classical music, romantic music cannot sustain the illusion of a universe of competent listeners.

On the other hand, the same characteristics that suggest a restriction of structural competence can also be interpreted in an obverse manner. Precisely because the romantic structure, if defined narrowly in temporal and, especially, tonal terms, does not seem to embody a whole self-evident meaning within itself, one can suppose that the romantic work points to other sorts of meaning which do not inhere in its temporal structure. In fact, romantic music, does seem to make explicit the possibility of another sort of musical competence, one that has a much greater resemblance to its counterpart in natural language than structural competence.

This second sort of competence, which I call stylistic competence, involves replacing the quasi-logical semiotic autonomy idealized in classicism with the literal breadth of a more concretely physical but semiotically incomplete sort of autonomy. In this connection it is useful to recall that in aesthetic judgment, as Kant presents it, cognitive weight is shifted from an insufficient faculty of understanding, which cannot sustain its own ostensible claim of a cognitively privileged status, to an openly contingent and concrete faculty of empirical perception, which neither contains nor leads to any one comprehensive or cognitively necessary interpretation. Unlike the classical structure, which evokes so powerfully the Kantian vision of a secure cognitive universality, the romantic musical structure seems explicitly designed as an object for the aesthetic judgment, with its far more manifest epistemological uncertainties. The romantic musical structure, that is, seems to present itself to the concrete subjective faculty of empirical perception (operating within concrete cultural limits) as an object which can be taken for autonomous only in the sense of having a physically fixed or static existence. Beyond asserting its condition as a physical (and humanly produced) structure, it makes no claim to an implicit meaning that must, out of objective necessity, be understood completely or deduced unmistakably over time. On the contrary, it gives concrete shape to a strong doubt that such unmistakable understanding is even possible. Accepting the irreducible contingency of perception as universal (and as a limiting condition of all apprehension), and conceding the contingency of the connections that may be made between perceptual meanings and a given semiotic structure, the romantic musical work seems to shift from an abstractly logical to an empirical, and in many ways linguistic, ideal of meaning, and to define itself through more or less broadly external features which, within arbitrary cultural limits, seem least likely to be missed.[21]

Thus, romantic music gives the impression of trying to compensate for the loss of the classical semiotic universe by reconstituting a semiotic universe of another sort. Unable any longer to simulate the *temporal* generation of a logically unified meaning out of a single tonal premise, the romantic piece seems to go about defining a universe of meaning in a *spatial* manner, by broadening the concept of musical structure. This it does by superimposing on its tonal structure, in a fashion that suggests the establishment of a series of analogous structures, what seem to be various other, autonomous layers of potential meaning. These may include nonmusical layers (titles, texts, programs). What is primarily involved, however, is a phenomenon of a sort already noted within the harmonic structure: an individuation of essentially nonimplicational musical parameters and their internal components, especially parameters other than harmony, such as melody, dynamics, and timbre—although one could also include purely coloristic aspects of harmony as examples of sonority in itself. The increased emphasis on these parameters could, admittedly, be interpreted as an attempt to clarify for the understanding, through the imposition of rhetoric (a term that I do not use pejoratively),[22] the rationality of the underlying tonal argument. The effect, however, is exactly the opposite, for this emphasis on the broad structure or total, concrete configuration and its self-contained, concrete details helps to obscure the temporal connections of tonal argument and to limit the role of the latter as a source of meaning. Thus it happens, precisely as in the case of purely structural analysis, that the listener finds himself pointed away from the temporal structure, in its evident semiotic inadequacy, to the possibility of a semiotic universe defined outside that structure and, ultimately, outside the music altogether.

To enter into such a universe or draw upon it as a source of meaning, the listener must be able to refer to what can be imagined as analogous, essentially stylistic structures, both cultural and individual, coexisting outside and yet somehow underneath the music. In making such reference, the listener can develop a type of competence whereby he is able, on the basis of static associations or isolated details, to recognize the musical structure as a whole in the sense that he can identify it: assign it a provenance and date, for example, or a composer, a particular history, even a name.[23] What this means, in essence, is that by renouncing the classical veneer of cognitive abstraction and reveling in the autonomy of music *as a concrete sensuous medium*, the romantic musical structure exposes far more clearly than the classical one a fundamental limitation that post-Kantian thought can begin to associate with all semiotic structures; it exposes the ultimate cognitive direction of man's semiotic structures as being not outward but backward or inward toward the particular archetypal structure or structures that project them.

This limitation is clear in the extent to which romantic music defines its own styles by evoking other musical styles. It is, perhaps, especially obvious in the massive efforts at structural autonomy that became so common during the nineteenth century, by which I mean those romantic works that seem to aspire quite literally to the grand size or systematic status of the physical universe, through a large-scale accumulation of nonimplicational devices that, again, often have some sort of important precedent in Beethoven. I think here of works that link their movements through cyclical returns or even through actual physical transitions (for example, Liszt's *Les Préludes*); of works with thematically retrospective perorations that seem more like rhetorical climaxes than logical syntheses (Mendelssohn's *Scottish* Symphony, for example, or even Wagner's overture to *Die Meistersinger*); of works that employ gargantuan orchestras (such as Strauss's *Also sprach Zarathustra*); and of works that incorporate or evoke a rich diversity of preexistent musical sources (for example, Mahler's First Symphony). The more the nineteenth-century work tries to encompass —and there may be some parallel here with the dialectical system through which Hegel overcomes Kant's disjunctions—the more evident it becomes that its boundaries remain limited by a determining subjectivity. To find anything close to a whole meaning in such works one is virtually thrust outside them into a kind of hermeneutical excavation for highly particular underlying sources. Mahler used the term *world* in connection with his symphonies; these works are indeed much larger and more ambitious with respect to diversity of content than any Mozart symphony. Yet for all its scope, Mahler's symphonic world has such an extraordinarily explicit personal and cultural particularity that it simply cannot project, even as a norm, the ideal of universal intelligibility and communication, except, perhaps, by way of the obvious absence of their possibility. Instead, through its extreme emphasis on style, it virtually spells out its fear of incomprehension of itself as an internally distinct structure, as well as the high degree of specific cultural information it requires for any sort of comprehension at all.

This is the sort of information that is involved in the notion of stylistic competence projected by romantic music; there is no doubt that with respect to the scope of communication, this sort of competence has certain advantages over the purely structural competence suggested by classicism, in large measure the advantages of linguistic competence. Thus, much of the knowledge needed for stylistic competence can be acquired passively (for example, by living within a culture or by hearing certain music constantly). Much of the rest of this knowledge, having a particular or empirical identity, can be learned (say, as discrete facts). Moreover, once gained, stylistic competence involves no active processes of reasoning; hence, competent stylistic descriptions can be made by many who are unable to produce the types of analysis, above all harmonic analysis, traditionally demanded of the structurally competent.

Stylistic meaning, however, clearly involves substantial semiotic disadvantages as well. First, the semiotic relations involved in stylistic meaning are openly contingent. This means that although a musical configuration, insofar as it has stylistic meaning, is without doubt formally governed by some configuration of particular subjective structures, the relationship between these two kinds of configuration is at most the disjunct relation of analogy and cannot be conclusively demonstrated.[24] Nor is there any certain way of knowing how close one has come to identifying all the layers in the configuration of governing subjective structures, let alone to "learning" that configuration itself. Consequently, stylistic meaning cannot be considered a meaning ever present in a musical structure, open to complete or secure reconstitution through an exercise of reason; rather, it is a meaning that must be assumed to be incompletely known at best, a meaning that can readily be severed or lost through historical time or distance, leaving the structure essentially meaningless to most. This is why romantic music, once it has emphasized stylistic elements of structure—elements that appeal primarily to sensory perception rather than to any quasi-conceptual sort of understanding—seems to be explicitly conceding the contingent relation of all meanings to structure, and even the possible imminent loss of its own meanings.

Furthermore, the competence associated with stylistic meaning is by definition a limited and partial mode of comprehension; for recognizing the physical identity of a whole structure, or that of its details, is not the same as following the formal connections within that whole. Indeed, stylistic competence may, in a peculiar sense, even preclude structural competence. For much as those who are fully competent to follow the course of an argument are less likely than the falteringly competent to perceive that argument consciously as an autonomous meaningful structure, so, too, conversely, the more compelled the listener is to experience a musical structure in terms of its stylistic or physical identity, or of elements that give it a particular identity, the less he seems compelled, or even permitted, to have the illusion of perceiving that structure as a temporally unified argument. And without question, it is a far greater misunderstanding of musical meaning to confuse the identities of two symphonies by a romantic stylist such as Brahms than two by the arch-classicist Haydn. In fact, a good deal of Romantic music seems to suggest, on the one hand, that neither structural nor stylistic competence is adequate by itself to understand a musical structure in its entirety, and on the other hand, that once the two are distinctly defined, it is virtually impossible to reintegrate them.[25] It is as if romantic music revealed a disjunction between these two autonomous yet incomplete modes of comprehension to be inherent in semiotic processes, precisely as the *Critique of Judgment* reveals such disjunctions as are inherent in the relationships between man's inner mental faculties and capacities, such as perception and understanding.

In the end, indeed, romantic music seems strongly to support the post-Kantian thesis that stylistic and structural understanding simply cannot be reconciled because of contradictions between the norm of physical autonomy, which precludes (as heteronomous) an intrinsic dependence on interpretation or on meaning, and the norm of semiotic autonomy, which promises objectively independent, or intrinsic, meaning. Although from the same post-Kantian standpoint it seems clear that the two norms have an analogous element in that each is defined by a concrete subjective faculty—the former, primarily, through perception, the latter, primarily, through understanding—nevertheless, it is an element that undercuts the distinctiveness of understanding, with its abstract norm of semiotic autonomy, leaving only perception, which makes no claim to universal validity, and its norm of physical autonomy, which, strictly speaking, rejects every vestige of intrinsic meaning. Thus again, though it would appear that stylistic concreteness of structure cannot, despite the promise of classical music, be fused in any knowable way into an identity with logical abstractness of structure, romantic music indicates that the latter can be subsumed under the former in a self-negating way or as an analogical variant of the former, which means, in either case, subsumed in a way that exposes the common reference of both perception and understanding, not to a purely abstract universal structure of reason but to an absence of universal or intrinsic meaning in any semiotic structure.[26] In its exposure of a disjunction between stylistic and structural kinds of competence, romantic music then seems openly to criticize the idealized classical universe, with its identity of stylistic perception and structural understanding, in much the same way as Kant's *Critique of Judgment* tacitly exposes as an illusion the possibility of an autonomous, in the sense of an implicitly intelligible, semiotic structure. What Kant inadvertently suggests, romantic music, with some self-consciousness, exemplifies: the contingency—and almost certain empirical impossibility—of a semiotic universe.

Before closing I should like to illustrate briefly some ways in which the general conception of musical romanticism developed here might be used in a specific

EXAMPLE 1

Prélude

F. Chopin. Op. 28, No. 2

critical interpretation. Let us take a small work that is instructive in that it crystallizes the characteristic elements of the romantic conception of autonomous musical structure with great vividness. I have in mind Chopin's "Second Prelude" for the piano, in A minor (example 1).

The work has no title, and few would deny that tonality figures in it in an important structural sense. By starting on the dominant minor, E, instead of on the tonic, A, and wending its way through a series of analogous or partly analogous harmonic patterns to a relatively brief cadence on the tonic, this piece raises fascinating questions about aspects of classical tonality that can, in a post-classical perspective, be grasped as problematical, for example, the logical necessity of assigning hierarchical precedence to (and, hence, cadencing in) one particular key. Moreover, every pitch in this piece has harmonic aspects that can, in retrospect, be related in some fashion to the tonal identity of the final cadence.

Nevertheless, this piece is hardly to be understood as the realization of any implication within an embodied premise concerning A minor. Thus, there is no way in which one can hear the movement from the opening of the piece to the closing as an essentially abstract, logical relationship that binds the piece in a self-evident fashion. In the first place, the opening triad of E minor defines a key which is tonally quite distant from the closing key, A, and which in fact bears a modal rather than tonally logical relationship to A minor or if it is put into a direct relationship with it or considered to be in the key of A. In actuality, however, the opening triad is never even heard in direct relationship to A minor. It is heard first as i in E minor, then as vi of G major, the first cadential key; but it can be identified as v (if, indeed, that is its function) only when the identity of the closing key is known, at the end of the piece. And by then, several harmonic disjunctions have separated "v" from "i," disjunctions that likewise keep the opening harmonic phrase from functioning as a premise. It is true that the first five measures after the opening two of introduction have roughly the shape of the antecedent-consequent structure so suggestive of a premise in classical music. Once the first full cadence is reached, however, on G, the unit is closed and implies nothing further.[27] To continue, the composer is forced to heighten the tension rhetorically by moving to a literally higher pitch, making a harmonically unprepared leap to a fairly distant triad, iii of G—significantly, the only link is one of pitch identity between the two Bs in the melody (bars 7-8)—where he then repeats, through the analogical device of transposition, the antecedent-consequent phrase up to its cadence.

Up to the deviation at that second cadence (bar 11), a repetitive pattern has been established, which one might expect to continue; if it did, the key reached in the next repetition would be A, the parallel major of the final key of the piece. But any such expectation is a response to the rhetorically induced momentum of repetition; it is not at all the same as the logical expectation of a structure that is sufficiently different in form (for instance, a complementary structure) to function as a resolution. On the contrary, there is no general form that could be conceived in advance as offering a proper close to the series initiated. Consequently, no propulsion is felt toward the key of A major (which in any case is tonally quite different from the A minor on which the piece actually ends); nor is there any reason to think that the next repetition of the pattern would be the last. Indeed, there is no reason to think of the empirical first phrase in this piece as the logically necessary first phrase of such a series. Leonard Meyer has characterized this opening phrase as "already part of a process."[28] Both in this sense and in terms of the divergence between the opening and the closing harmonies, one could well describe this piece as essentially beginning somewhere in its own harmonic middle. It certainly lacks not only the clear bounding framework of a single, unmistakable tonic key but also the clear outer boundaries of function and the corollary effect of intrinsic wholeness associated with the quasi-logical structure of premise-and-resolution.

Because no logical sort of implication is set up at the start of this piece, the breaking of the harmonic pattern at the end of the second phrase (bars 11-12) is not experienced as the kind of deviation from implied progress that increases propulsiveness toward a goal. Nor does the passage between the second and third phrases (bars 12-14) constitute a propulsive drive toward resolution in the same sense as a classical development section moves toward resolution. Instead, the effect of a disjunction is heightened and prolonged by the sudden exposure of especially harsh and largely unresolved dissonances in the bass pattern; by the arbitrary drop of the left-hand pattern to a different and lower version of the same chord (bars 12-13); and by the suspension of harmonic movement over a diminished-seventh chord, the most unsettled but also the most ambiguous of harmonies and, hence, the least logically implicative harmony in terms of any specific goal. Admittedly, this passage is at the same time rhetorically smoothed over by the conjunction of the downward movement of the bass, the fading of volume after a preceding rise, and the early entrance (analyzed below) of the next melodic phrase in the right hand (bar 14), so that on grounds other than those of harmonic implication or of any sort of temporal self-generation, the passage between bars 11 and 15 can be interpreted as signifying the rise and fall of uncertainty as a kind of imposed effect (with the fall continuing through most of the remainder of the piece). But neither these techniques nor the last-minute introduction of a harmonically resolving gesture (that is, of an augmented-sixth chord resolving to a six-four chord in bars 14-15) can overcome entirely the effect of a harmonic disjunction between the second and third phrases. One still has the sense that the diminished harmony breaks off to be replaced by the resumption of an arbitrary repetitive pattern at a harmonically arbitrary (though rhetorically plausible) point. Leonard Meyer sums up the impression of a lack of harmonic necessity at this supposed juncture when he notes, "It seems perfectly clear that any technical explanation of measures 12 to 16 purely in terms of harmonic goals and modulations must be inadequate."[29]

Finally, the last cadence, in A minor, does not serve as a logical goal of harmonic motion in the same sense that a tonic chord relieves the tension of a dominant pedal. Again, given the absence of a preceding clear implication of A minor, the final triad cannot have such a function; it can only be heard retrospectively as constituting the actual closing point of the piece, something quite different. Moreover, even within itself, the last segment of the piece (bars 14-23) does not define unmistakable movement toward a harmonic destination. For one thing, the dominant triad on E, which is needed to secure A minor as a harmonic goal, does not appear until two measures before the end (bar 21). To be sure, the six-four position of the first A-minor triad in this segment (bar 15) does differentiate that triad from its earlier counterparts (E minor, bar 1, B minor, bar 8), and thereby suggests a potentially significant change of direction. Initially, however, the change defines simply a relation of identity or difference to earlier elements, not the approach to an inevitable harmonic conclusion. The anticipatory harmonic function of the six-four triad of A minor becomes clear only in retrospect.

It is true that a six-four triad in an unambiguous harmonic context—for example, immediately preceding the cadenza in a classical concerto movement—can strongly imply a closing tonic; and one might, on the basis of this external historical information, predict the resolution of Chopin's six-four triad to one in root position. Even then, as already suggested elsewhere, one could not be certain in advance, on purely internal or harmonic grounds, that such a root-position triad would define an ultimate goal, or true tonic, rather than another intermediate one. Moreover, despite the familiarity of the harmonic device from classical practice, the effect of the six-four chord in the prelude is different, for the harmonic context here is not unambiguous. On the contrary, the melodic line tends at first to pull away from A minor toward B-flat major: the F in bar 17, which is left unharmonized, suggests, by analogy with its counterparts in bars 5 and 10, the dominant of B-flat. Even in bar 20, the grace note F, which contrasts strikingly with the F-sharp in bar 5, does not portend a tonic with the same propulsiveness as does a Beethovenian lowered-sixth degree; and here, too, as in bar 17, the melodic line literally resists harmonization. (It is by no means inconceivable that this latter F-natural, the sole note distinguishing the melodic pattern and pitch level of bar 20 from those of bar 5, could be denied tonal significance and exposed emphatically as a mere variance in pitch through a resumption of the earlier harmonic goal, G major.)

At any rate, the harmonic identity of bars 15-20 is sufficiently uncertain as to deprive the pedal points on E and A in bars 15-16 of a classically definitive V-I cadential function. Here the two notes seem part of a nonpropulsive, nondirectional, or, at most, ambivalent harmonic pattern, an impression strengthened by the dissolution of the octave on A in bars 15-16 into a sixth on A and F in bars 18-19, by the unresolved alternation of the A-minor triad, at this latter point, with the dissonant notes B and F, and by the blurring effect of the single sustaining-pedal indication.

Without doubt, the final cadence on A minor does put an actual (and plausibly rational) end to all preceding harmonic uncertainty; but rather than constituting the one possible end to the piece, it is a forcible and contingent end, more rhetorical than harmonically logical in its persuasiveness. Even the clear link between the melodic D and F in the last segment (bars 18-19) and the D and F-sharp in the first segment (bars 4-5) involves identity and difference, or arbitrary repetition and variance, rather than implication and resolution. Moreover, the momentum of the bass pattern is definitively broken not by harmonic resolution but by literal silence (bar 19). And finally, the prolonged dynamic diminuendo as well as the *slentando* and *sostenuto* markings (bars 18 and 21), the prolongation of the final V and I chords indicated by the arpeggiation signs, and the closing fermata—all, clearly imposed rhetorical markings—are essential as physical or empirical calming effects to render the final cadence fully coherent as a functional close to the piece.

In fact, this is a piece in which the conception of harmony as a force for constructing a continuous whole has given way to a preoccupation with problems of harmonic identity. Harmonic meaning in the sense of recognizable harmonic function is not absent in this piece, but by and large, harmonic structure has disintegrated into localized and roughly (though not in every respect audibly) analogous harmonic units.[30] These can be designated roughly as bars 1 to 7, 8 to 12, and 13 to the end. Each unit presents comparable progressions; each is seemingly involved in the attempt to wrest a harmonic identity out of harmonic ambiguity; and thus, each can be characterized as calling attention to the question of what it is, rather than as pointing temporally forward in a kind of semiotic metaphor to what it might mean. To be sure, there are harmonic differences among these units in terms of both their large-scale inner patterns and their chromatic and other detail; in particular, the last segment is distinctive in that it moves into its eventual key from an unstable harmony, stays in its key longer than the earlier phrases do, and is threatened by independent harmonic implications in the melody. Still, because of certain clear overall similarities of shape provided by harmony and even more by nonharmonic parameters, and because of the perceptible gaps between these units, these differences are experienced far less as differences of harmonic function in relation to a temporal whole than as differences in the actuality and the quality of particular identity.

This is not to say that the total configuration is harmonically incoherent and to be dismissed as irrational. Clearly, tonality is still being used to an extent in this piece to convey the sense that something happens in time. And without question it is possible to provide one's own semiotic connections between the segments of this piece and, therefore, to render a plausible account of the piece in terms of its temporal structure; nevertheless, the interpretation that results is very likely to involve an undercutting of the temporal dimension of this piece.[31] Therefore, the emphasis on the individual identity of the component phrases seems to encourage, or at least allows, one to construe this piece, in a kind of nontemporal, quasi-spatial sense, as an inventory of a few highly individualized aspects of an entity called *A minor*, an effect that is emphasized by the four distinctly different harmonizations (or nonharmonizations) of the cadential dotted-note patterns in bars 6-7, 11-12, 18-19, and 21-22. As a harmonic sort of meaning, of course, this is considerably more restricted than the impression of a self-embodied totality of generally valid meanings that a classical structure might seem to develop out of an A-minor proposition. Again, the piece projects the sense of being a harmonic fragment, a sense that is in one way confirmed by its extreme brevity, which seems to acknowledge renunciation of any large-scale constructive force inherent in tonality.

In short, Chopin's A-minor prelude is not without harmonic meaning, but the meaning does not present itself as a complete meaning. By the same token, not all of the meaning in this piece seems to inhere in its temporal harmonic structure. Melody, for example, makes a relatively independent contribution to the coherence of this piece by projecting its own disjunct pattern of analogues, one that differs from the harmonic pattern in overall shape (the melodic pattern is resumed at bar 14 with much smaller differences than those in the final harmonic pattern) and in harmonic identity (from bar 14 to the end). (On the whole, the pattern of analogues is more consistently audible in the melodic than in the harmonic structure of this piece; much of the structural clarity of the prelude depends on the ease with which similarities and differences in the melodic analogues can be retained over its relatively brief duration.) Though the relation of melody and harmony has significance in this piece, it is a relation that consists largely in coexisting differences of particular identity; in no sense can the harmony be said to imply the melody. Instead, one can begin to form an idea here of a total musical configuration consisting in an indeterminate number of relatively discrete, though potentially analogous, layers of structural significance that are not grounded in an implicit and unifying tonal premise. Such a configuration can be "explained" only in the sense that it can be imagined as originating in some individualized archetype of a rational configuration existing outside of the piece itself in the mind of the composer.

Likewise, pitch level (the rise to the first transposition of the pattern, bar 8, and the gradual falling from bar 12 on), the prolonged harshness of dissonance mid-piece (bars 10-14), dynamics (the implied rise to bar 12[32] and subsequent fall), tempo and touch markings, and literal silence (the rest over the falling bass in bar 13, the sudden cessation of the accompaniment in bars 17 and 20, and the complete break before the final melodic phrase in bar 19)—all define a pattern of rise and fall that becomes very common in romantic music as the constructive power of pure harmony weakens. This pattern of rhetorical emphasis, clearly a fundamental source of coherence in this piece, is used to reinforce harmonic uncertainty and closing, but it is no mere function of tonality. On the contrary, unlike the tonally generated dynamic of the classical structure, this essentially static pattern of internal rise and fall is imposed on the harmony, so to speak, precisely because it offers in physical terms a continuity that no longer has a quasi-logical counterpart in the disjunct harmonic pattern. In some ways this temporally "imposed" rhetoric is more integral to the structure of the piece than is the harmony. This seems especially so in the last segment, at bars 14-15, where the almost isolated falling bass patterns seem not to need the older harmonic and melodic patterns. The last return of these patterns (with the harmony altered) seems thrust upon the rhetorically flagging energies of the piece, pushed in arbitrarily as if in passing—an effect heightened by the rhythmic and harmonic anticipation in the precipitate melodic entrance (bar 14) that follows a prolonged melodic pause,[33] and an effect that, while literally narrowing the gap between the second and third phrases, adds also to the sense of disjunction between phrases already noted with respect to the harmony. Here again one is faced with the coexistence of discrete, though in some respects analogous, musical parameters that intensify consciousness of the presence of an outside source from which they must emanate.

Still another element that seems to give this piece a kind of sense independent of a tonal argument is its high degree of coloristic particularity. This particularity is provided first of all at the level of harmonic detail, for example, through the complexity and pervasive dissonance of the chromatic sonorities (which no amateur could comfortably analyze), and through the constant small changes in sonority and symmetry, as well as through the pervasive ambiguity of major and minor sonorities, both of which can be effected by differences of one or two notes.[34] The breaking of common rules, such as the resolution of dissonance[35] and even the avoidance of parallel octaves[36] also adds to the effect of coloristic particularity, as do the use of a fairly low range of the piano and the close, thick spacing of the individual pitches. Along with the relentlessness of ostinato rhythm and the percussivness of the constant pianistic attack on pairs of low-pitched notes, which is softened for only one moment by the sustaining pedal, the chromatic and pianistic sonorities of this piece give it the meaning that is almost surely the one most often attached to it—its character of harshness as a total configuration.

This is a kind of meaning, however, that must be called stylistic, in my sense, in that it points attention forcibly away from the internal structural connections of the piece to other sources of meaning, such as the entire set of preludes, and, beyond that, Chopin's style; for it is only in terms of its somewhat exceptional character relative to these latter that this harshness of identity can be said to make full sense. And indeed, the contrast of sonorities and textures among the various preludes is a principal source of intelligibility for them all. But it should be noted that the entire set of preludes does not bear the same relationship of implication or reciprocity to the individual preludes that seems to connect part and whole in a classical work; thus, unlike the system of tonality in classicism, the whole set cannot be said to inhere in any of the individual works (except, perhaps, in the odd sense that the key arrangement of the entire set might be needed to secure positive identification of the tonic in the "Second Prelude"). Instead, the set must be acknowledged as external to the individual prelude and as related to it only in a contingent fashion. One could say that the set seems something like a contingent analogue of a piece such as the second prelude, since the set, too, consists in a nontemporal, quasi-spatial inventory of discrete, analogous components.

In its presentation of preludes in each of the twenty-four keys, the set is actually a romantic attempt at a systematic structure. But just as the configuration of each prelude cannot in any way be taken as a set of abstractly logical, generalizable, or intrinsically "true" relationships, so, too, the "system" here is far more openly particular than classical tonality and, hence, far less easily interpreted as the embodiment of a universally accessible, abstractly meaningful structure. Unlike classical tonality (or any natural language), the cycle of preludes is completely and empirically fixed in its structure, and its expressive possibilities (though not the interpretations that can be applied to it) are inalterably finite. In other words, no further manipulation of this system is possible, because as a *langue*, so to speak, the cycle is nothing more general than the sum of its *paroles*, or individual preludes; like the "Second Prelude" and its component phrases, the cycle, too, seems more concerned with autonomous identity than with implicit meaning of structure. To be sure, the empirical contingency of its particular character may well send the listener to a more general source of identification or meaning, such as Chopin's style, or, in the case of a scholar, a still broader configuration of romantic style. But again, neither individual nor cultural style constitutes the sort of system that one could imagine deducing from either the individual prelude or the cycle. In terms of the second prelude, then, all of these broader structures—set, style, cultural movement—can be construed as providing legitimate sources of meaning for those who already know them or know how to look for them; but they cannot be designated a single, cohesive meaning that is completely embodied in the "Second Prelude."

It seems fair to say that through a work as seemingly autonomous as the "Second Prelude," Chopin makes what is in effect a post-Kantian critique of the norm of the autonomous semiotic universe idealized in classicism. It even seems symptomatic of the limitations that such a critique sets upon man's semiotic structures that this apparently pure musical structure has been cited for its qualities of "doubt and uncertainty,"[37] not only in the essentially formal terms of Leonard Meyer's criticism, that mixture of poetic and technical terms (itself indicative of romantic attitudes towards musical autonomy) that typifies so many nineteenth-century interpretations, such as this one, called "Presentiment of Death":

> This is as uncertain in character as in key. It begins in E-minor, goes into G-major, then to B-minor, only to lose itself slowly in A-minor. The mood is constantly changing, yet it always comes back to one and the same thought, the melancholy tolling of a funeral knell. The two-voiced accompaniment in the left-hand is difficult to play legato. The right hand bears the inexorable voice of death, though toward the end it falters and loses the measure in

uncertain tones, as if saying, "He comes not, the deliverer! It was a delusion." This is what the questioning end seems to say.[38]

From the accounts of both Meyer and von Bülow, one could guess that Chopin has captured in this piece something of the contingency surrounding all semiotic objects. And just as this piece seems to involve the relationship of analogy in its temporal segmentation, its layering of semiotic parameters, and its reference to its parent work and stylistic origins, so, too, it would seem that the construction of vastly different interpretations by Meyer and von Bülow around the common notion of uncertainty provides good evidence of the analogical relationships at work in acts of criticism.

Notes

1. On types of sonata movement see Charles Rosen, *The Classical Style* (New York: Norton, 1972), pp. 99-100.

2. On counterparts to a *signifié* in baroque music see Manfred Bukofzer, "Allegory in Baroque Music," *Journal of the Warburg and Courtauld Institutes* 3 (1939-40): 2-4, 20-21.

3. See, for example, Douglas Hofstadter, *Gödel, Escher, Bach: An Eternal Golden Braid* (New York: Basic Books, 1979), p. 458.

4. Reference in the following discussion to Kant's critical philosophy is based largely on a close analysis of the *Critique of Judgment*, both in English translation and in German. See Immanuel Kant, *Critique of Judgment*, trans. J. H. Bernard (New York: Hafner, 1951) (hereafter cited as *CJ*), and *Kritik der Urtheilskraft*, ed. Königlich Presussischen Akademie der Wissenschaften, Kant's *Gesammelte Schriften*, vol. 5 (Berlin: G. Reimer, 1913). My analysis is not, by and large, one of his own intended meanings but rather one of those that, in retrospect, seem to me inherent in his argument.

5. As with any system, that is, no amount of theoretically rational internal consistency can establish the rationality of the system as a whole.

6. See, for example, *CJ*, section 34, page 128, where Kant argues, in effect, that the job of art criticism is to refer various configurations back to the structure of judgment to see if the apprehension of these configurations involves a state of internal analogy (between the capacities for perception and for comprehension) within the structure of judgment. That criticism, however, can never locate or define the common structure underlying all actual, individual faculties of judgment or, hence, deduce "correct" judgments of beauty from such an archetype. (Hereafter, references to the *Critique of Judgment* will omit the words "section" and "page" and simply cite the number of each, separated by a colon. Section numbers in Roman numerals refer to the Preface.) For another formulation of the epistemological problem broached here see my article "The Cultural Message of Musical Semiology: Some Thoughts on Music, Language, and Criticism since the Enlightenment," *Critical Inquiry* 4 (1978): 749, especially the following statement and its attendant footnote: "in calling attention to the dependence of objective knowledge on language, Kant had provided a basis for questioning the objectivity of the knowledge obtained through language, that is, for doubting the power of language to reach any such objective truth as did exist."

7. On problems connected with the notion of cultural structures see especially Bukofzer, "Allegory in Baroque Music," p. 1; Charles Rosen, "The Origins of Walter Benjamin," *New York Review of Books* 24 (10 November 1977): 33-34; and E. D. Hirsch, *The Aims of Interpretation* (Chicago: University of Chicago, 1976), pp. 46-49.

8. The sorts of meanings I am assuming to be imposed on semiotic structures comprise what could in broad terms be called *perceptual* meanings (static structural wholeness and "surface" detail as they are perceived or recognized by the interpreter) and *conceptual* meanings (internal connections that are imagined to lie at a "deeper" internal level of the semiotic structure than surface detail, a level from which they must be extracted in a temporal process of following or reconstituting connections, which amounts to an exercise of discursive understanding). This distinction between types of meaning implies a

distinction between perception and understanding, the dual "moments" that Kant locates in the faculties of both cognition and aesthetic judgment (albeit with certain differences, as evidenced in *CJ* 59: 197 and also in Hirsch, *Aims of Interpretation*, p. 75).

On the basis of my analysis of Kant's third critique, I am in fact positing such a distinction, not only because the two capacities define themselves according to relatively different norms, but also because, as Kant makes explicit in the case of aesthetic judgment, understanding cannot, through any absolute cognitive status, absorb and negate the contingencies of sensory perception, any more than a necessary connection can be established in any cognitively absolute sense between a sensory perception and a given cognitive interpretation that is attached to it. At the same time, however, both perception and understanding turn out to be concrete and subjective, and hence, cognitively contingent faculties, so that with respect to cognitive value, there seems to be no *significant* difference between them. In short, as in Kant's account of judgment, the two moments appear to be distinct or disjunct in the manner of analogy: they are irreconcilable, and yet not significantly different, with each, in a sense, containing its own moments of perception and interpretation.

Clearly, perceptual meaning becomes acknowledged as a kind of archetype for cognitive sorts of meaning in nineteenth-century music, precisely as it does in the faculty of judgment, where, by Kant's account, the cognitive value of understanding is undermined openly and shifted, essentially, onto perception, which has its own interpretative moment (see *CJ*, 35: 129: "comprehension" [*Zusammenfassung*]). This shift could be said to signify a transition from a cultural preference for cognition, with its inviolable moment of understanding, as the archetypal cognitive (and semiotic) faculty, to a preference in this respect for aesthetic judgment, which in effect not only puts cognitive weight on a sensory moment—perception—but also makes explicit the ultimate dependence of understanding in *both* cognition and judgment on a cognitively problematical, and no more than aesthetically "verifiable," transcendental structure of reason. In other words, the shift of cognitive weight to perception seems to involve recognition of precisely the same sort of relation between cognition and aesthetic judgment as that noted above between understanding and perception, the latter member being archetypal in each case. See also below, n. 14 and n. 26.

9. Rosen, *The Classical Style*, p. 100.

10. Ibid., p. 33.

11. This is essentially Leonard Meyer's point when, in connection with a harmonic digression in the finale of Mozart's Symphony no. 39, he observes that no general rules can be made for particular musical events; he is pointing out the absence of logical determinism within individually designed semiotic structures. See *Explaining Music* (Berkeley and Los Angeles: University of California Press, 1973), pp. 10-12.

12. Jacques Barzun, *Classic, Romantic, and Modern* (Garden City, N.Y.: Anchor 1961), p. 38.

13. See *CJ*, 53: 174; also Walter Serauky, *Die musikalische Nachahmungsästhetik im Zeitraum von 1700 bis 1850* (Münster: Helios-Verlag, 1929), pp. 5-6.

14. See especially *CJ*, 22:78, 35:129, and 57:185. It should be noted here that although Kant associates aesthetic judgment with the sublime as well as with the beautiful, I have throughout this discussion construed that structure of judgment manifested in determinations of beauty as archetypal for all aesthetic judgment, a construction I believe warranted within the *Critique of Judgment*. I would further argue that in spite of Kant's indication to the contrary (*CJ*, 1:37, n. 1), the structure of judgment associated with beauty actually suggests itself in the *Critique of Judgment* as archetypal for every sort of judgment considered by Kant in this work, including teleological judgment and even determinant (that is, logical or objective cognitive) judgment.

15. See especially *CJ*, 22:78, 35:129, and 57:185. On the whole, in the *Critique of Judgment*, cognition points toward two discrete realms, subjectivity and objectivity, though it cannot link them with cognitive security and in the end can define them only as analogous forms within a single realm, subjectively. This latter sort of definition is the normative condition within aesthetic judgment, which offers no illusion of a connection between the subjective and objective worlds, and which, even within subjectivity, isolates perception in the sense that it can refer a specific percept to no specific concept of the understanding (though it can refer it to a state of analogy between the faculties of perception and understanding). Assuming that the aesthetic structure, as argued here, replaces the cognitive as the archetypal semiotic structure, one can plot a progress from the complementary dualities that seem necessarily connectable through cognition to the state of intrastructural and contingent analogy, which appears actually to obtain in cognition as well as in aesthetic judgment, to the potential isolation of the fundamentally aesthetic percept. Such a progress is highly suggestive as a model for the history of musical structure in classicism, romanticism, and post-romantic formalism, respectively.

16. Cf. Rosen's assertion that Schlegel and Novalis turn criticism from an act of judgment into an act of understanding ("The Ruins of Walter Benjamin," *New York Review of Books* 24 [27 October 1977]: 32).

17. If classical syntax suggests logical deduction, these cumulative processes seem more akin to empirical deduction. Clearly, there is some sort of analogical relationship between the suggestion of empirical induction at this level of temporal structure in romantic music and the suggestion, in this same music, of the need for an accumulation or series of analogical interpretations to approach a total understanding of a semiotic structure, a suggestion brought about through stress on what will be called "stylistic meaning"; see also Hofstadter, *Gödel, Escher, Bach*, p. 582.

18. A good place in Beethoven's works to observe many elements of the techniques noted here is in the first movement of the *Waldstein* Sonata op. 53.

19. On the whole, this is likewise so if competence is defined as the ability to perform rather than as the ability to comprehend.

20. See Friedrich Blume, *Classic and Romantic Music*, trans. M. D. Herter Norton (New York: Norton, 1970), pp. 108-9, on the transformation of all critics of romantic music into dilettantes.

21. Though in a sense it may seem strange to equate this sort of surface perception with linguistic competence, it is precisely the point of this discussion to suggest that even ostensibly cognitive semiotic structures, such as those making an ordinary use of language, engage at most faculties of concretely logical apprehension which, like perception, operate by analogy with structures in subjective, concretely defined minds and, thus, are cognitively no more verifiable or secure than the faculty of perception.

22. There is, indeed, a rather broad school of thought today that, without embracing irrationalism, is trying to redefine reason concretely, in terms quite different from those of traditional Western cognitive theory, by directing attention to sensuous devices (such as rhetoric) and perception, much as romantic music itself can be construed as trying to do. See, for example, Chaim Perelman and Lucie Olbrechts-Tyteca, *The New Rhetoric: A Treatise on Argumentation*, trans. John Wilkinson and Purcell Weaver (Notre Dame, Ind.: University of Notre Dame Press, 1969), beginning with the remarks on pp. 2-4, which define an attack on "the idea of self-evidence as characteristic of reason" (p. 3). See also Claude Lévi-Strauss, *The Savage Mind* (Chicago: University of Chicago Press, 1966); and my own article "Kant, Adorno, and the Self-Critique of Reason: Towards a Model for Music Criticism," *Humanities in Society* 2 (1979): 353-85. In a sense, of course, the *Critique of Judgment* is itself an attempt to secure the rationality of the aesthetic on grounds other than the strictly cognitive which would yet satisfy certain rational requirements of cognition; see especially 15:64, where the absence of cognitive value in an aesthetic judgment is admitted, and 9:51-53, 57:184-86, and 59: 197-200, where, in effect, Kant offers compensation for that absence.

23. This is not, clearly, an unconscious apprehension of wholes, where one knows the end has been reached because one has understood an internal rational argument, but a conscious perception of wholes, where one recognizes the end from isolated "external" cues—or from previous hearings.

24. (In essence this is what Hofstadter means when he asserts that "hiddenness is of the essence in semantic properties" [*Gödel, Escher, Bach*, p. 583].) This relationship defines a clear instance of that paradoxical state of autonomy to which the *Critique of Judgment* calls attention, in which a structure is at once free of and dependent on a governing mind. In connection with the relative advantages and disadvantages of stylistic competence, it is worth pointing out that Berlioz, an archetypical romantic critic, vacillated continually concerning the benefits and limitations of education for an understanding of romantic music. The cultural significance of this vacillation is analyzed with great insight in a forthcoming doctoral dissertation on Berlioz and Delacroix, entitled "The Romantic Artist's Dilemma," written by Kineret Jaffe, a student in the History of Culture Committee at the University of Chicago.

25. Thus, though more Western listeners today probably have some stylistic competence in romantic music than in any other style of art music, few have structural competence; conversely, the formalism of most contemporary analysis exemplifies a loss of access to distinctive nineteenth-century modes of hearing and meanings. See Carl Dahlhaus, "Fragmente zur musikalischen Hermeneutik," *Beiträge zur musikalischen Hermeneutik*, ed. C. Dahlhaus, Studien zur Musikgeschichte des 19 Jahrhunderts, vol. 43 (Regensburg: G. Bosse, 1975), p. 161, and "Thesen über Programmusik," ibid., p. 189.

26. Given the central importance of analogy in *Critique of Judgment*, it is worth noting that the relationship described here between understanding and perception is in some ways precisely analogous to that described by Kant in his third critique, between the theoretical, or nature, and the moral, or freedom (II:12, and IX:32).

27. In fact, the two melodic phrases in bars 3-4 and 5-7 are actually analogous variants. See example 1 of the analysis from Leonard Meyer's *Emotion and Meaning in Music*, as reprinted in the Norton Critical

Score of Chopin's *Preludes, Op. 28*, ed. Thomas Higgins (New York: Norton, 1973), p. 76. Here the relationship of analogy seems graphically indicated, though Meyer himself characterizes it simply as a relationship of similarity. Again, although the "Second Prelude" represents a harmonic extreme in relation to the other preludes, the latter can likewise be analyzed fruitfully in terms of analogy, identity-difference, and arbitrary succession; and, of course, other nineteenth-century works (Beethoven's Ninth Symphony, Schuman's *Dichterliebe*, Wagner's *Tristan und Isolde*) present harmonically ambiguous openings.

28. Meyer, *Preludes*, p. 79.

29. Ibid., p. 78.

30. See the comparison of the harmonic structure of bars 12-23 with that of the earlier and shorter segments, as analyzed by Meyer, *Preludes*, p. 78; again, Meyer himself describes the relationship simply in terms of similarity.

31. This aspect of my analysis obviously differs from the emphasis in Meyer's analysis on aspects of process; yet, to the extent that process can be distinguished from implication, the two analyses need not be mutually exclusive. What I am suggesting, in effect, is that processes of change that call attention to particular states of identity or difference rather than submerging themselves in generally established functional patterns tend to undermine their own temporal force. Change is not the same as movement.

32. On the implied rise see Thomas Higgins, "Notes Toward a Performance with References to the Valldemosa Autograph," in the Norton Critical Score of Chopin's *Preludes*, p. 62.

33. The effect of anticipation itself at this point represents an audible intensification of an analogous effect of anticipation at the beginning of the previous melodic phrase. Whereas the first melodic phrase enters on the first beat of the third measure on the same harmony that has been established in the first two measures of introduction—a harmony that appears to be more or less stable—the second phrase comes in (bar 8) on the second beat of its measure, after only half a measure of the new harmony involved. (As a transposition of the opening chord, this harmony is clearly the analogue of its predecessor, though its stability is now, by example, open to a doubt that is subsequently justified.) The last principal melodic phrase enters (bar 14) before the unstable diminished-seventh chord has resolved into a new version (now in six-four rather than root position) of the relatively stable chord that opened the piece. And though the bass pattern over which the melodic phrase enters has been going for a full measure before the melodic entrance, the first note of the melody does not wait this time for the second beat of the measure but comes in on the rhythmically weak, second half of the first beat of its own measure. Hence, by comparison with its counterpart in bar 8, the first melodic note in bar 14 seems to have entered too early, both in harmonic and in melodic terms.

34. This piece is a fine example of the narrowing down to units of one or two notes of the expressive burden in much romantic music.

35. Not only is it possible to view the whole piece as an avoidance of the logical resolution of harmonically inconclusive points of internal rest but also the constant reassertion of dissonance on a more localized level undercuts the very notion of resolution. In at least one critical instance, moreover, the rhetorical disruption of the resolving process is so striking that it undermines the connectedness and logical authority of a harmonically "correct" resolution and even suggests the latter as the breach of a rhetorical norm. I refer to the E-major triad of bar 21, which cannot fully counterbalance the pointedness with which the last bass-line dissonances and the accompanying pedal, in bars 18 and 19, are broken off, or differentiate itself completely from the fundamental E, which permeates that dissonant blur.

36. Note the accented octave progression from E to D in bars 3-4, etc.

37. Meyer, *Preludes*, p. 78.

38. "Chopin's Preludes, op. 28, Analyzed by von Bülow," trans. Frederick S. Law, *The Musician* 16 (February 1911): 88. These analyses cannot be ascribed with complete certainty to von Bülow since they were transcribed by a pupil, Laura Rappoldi-Kahrer; in any case, the fundamental point here is unaffected. I am grateful to Susan T. Sommer of the New York Public Library for locating these notes to the "Preludes" on short notice.

6

Music Criticism:
Practice and Malpractice

KARL ASCHENBRENNER

Introduction

IT WILL COME AS NO SURPRISE if I express the opinion that music criticism is in something of a state of crisis, seeing that government, the economy, education, morality, and the arts are in similar state. As in some of these other areas, one can detect a kind of suspense of action, in which what has always been recognized as the proper task of the enterprise has not been performed, and often a kind of permissiveness has tended to prevail. Since the face of the arts has changed so radically, it is not surprising that the criticism of it has seemed to lose its bearings. Critics have either been afraid to expect and demand of the arts what they did at an earlier time or have been unable to formulate or reformulate their expectations for the current scene. The purpose of this essay is to determine just what role criticism can and should play.

Some of what I say will apply to arts other than music but I invite your attention particularly to music and to particular musical examples, whether these are explicitly mentioned or not. The crisis in music criticism is directly bound up with the critical state of the arts and prevails wherever current artistic practice tends to move to a point almost directly opposite from where the arts were at the beginning of this century. From heroes we have gone to antiheroes, from arts to antiarts; but one is little likely to have anticriticism. Rather, one will have criticism that is unsure of how to deal with a situation that it has seemingly never before faced. However, I cannot here deal equally with the state of the arts and the state of criticism. For the former I will rely largely on the readers' undoubted familiarity with the unusual spectacles or presentations one encounters in art museums and in avant-garde centers for new music or drama. The audience and spectators are bewildered, rather than hostile, as they were earlier in the century. Instead, those who witness these events are inclined toward a certain docility, that is, in its original sense, a willingness to be taught and to apprehend the objects of attention in accordance with whatever intention can be discerned in them. With such open-mindedness, today's audience might also be ready to gain from the critic whatever guidance he may offer, if only he knew what to say.

The practice-malpractice phrase I have used can be used in either of two senses, which I will perhaps somewhat oversimplify as the *descriptive* and the *prescriptive*. The title of this essay may appear to promise a descriptive survey of contemporary criticism, particularly in music, but this is far too large a task to carry out in such a limited time. Moreover, it would necessarily have to be selective and thus might present criticism in a better or worse light than it deserves. I have elsewhere devoted some effort to ascertain empirically the kinds of things critics of many stripes say, and I will not repeat them here, except incidentally.[1] My attention is therefore focused in the prescriptive direction to try to see just what I think music criticism virtually has to be and ought to be, regardless of the actual, and no doubt passing, current complexion of music. I should also say that I am concerned almost wholly with criticism directed toward the composer's rather than the performer's work. The latter must always presuppose the former. Since the select roster of the great works of the past seems practically canonical by now, it is criticism of new work, criticism in the fire or the frying pan of the present that I have in mind.[2]

The Need for Criticism

Perhaps one of our first questions should be, "Criticism, who needs it?" The composer's attitude is likely to be, "Not I. If the critic tells me my work is a masterpiece, I like to hear it, but it is of course something I already know. If he says it is mediocre or poor, he is of course miserably mistaken." Let us then consider the audience. I will give you a kind of parable. When I entered college I betook myself to the elementary course in economics. The name of the text, as I recall, and the theme of the opening lecture, was "production economics." The lecturer explained that in the economic process the center of the action was production, with an entailed subordinate process of distribution. Perhaps, said he, we would be likely to link the terms 'production' and 'consumption' and to think the latter was as important as the former. Not so. Consumption, that is, what the consumer does with the product, is of no economic importance to the producer of the commodity; what matters is that the product is bought. Of all that I heard in the following weeks, it seems only this remained. Since then, the interest of the producer in the sale of products has of course scarcely diminished. But we also hear much of consumerism, and this has made itself felt to such a degree that I doubt that that old lecture would be so casually repeated in current freshman courses.

But in the current musical scene the producers have a curiously similar response to those economists. As reported in the press, Virgil Thomson recently said that "music in any generation is not what the public thinks of it, but what the musicians make of it. . . . The lay public has no responsibility at all toward music."[3] One can in-terpret this statement in such a way as to find truth in it, but it also betrays a rather lofty attitude that has been typified by most artists of our time. Production alone is important, the artist seems to say, or, in the vernacular, the public be damned. It is of no consequence to us, the composers, whether or not you the public like what we are doing, so long as you are diligent in furnishing the funds to sustain us. Thus the artist, perversely, I think, keeps deepening his alienation from the audience instead of showing concern to deepen all the dimensions of musical culture by his contribu-tion to it and offering us invincible reasons why we should attend to his work. One can gauge the depth dimension of this culture and its depth potentialities when we witness the response of nearly all audiences to the concert rendition of, let us say, the classics of the period 1700-1850. A public with that much good sense deserves to be consulted.

I do not wish to make a complete identification of the musical public with the economic consumer or to ask that the composer simply tailor his goods to fit the client. But if he is not seeking to gain the favor of the audience, to regain a sense of oneness with them, to speak for them, express their thoughts and feelings, their anxieties and raptures, why does he ask us to attend to him at all? He has often sulked in disappointment with the current audience and insisted that he is sure of the approbation of generations yet unborn—the latter is in fact a rare phenomenon if there is no approbation in the lifetime of the artist.[4]

It is at this juncture that the critic must play a role. He is the mediator, but like all fair mediators he must face both the composer and the audience and be able to speak for and against both of them. At a recent conference of composers and critics at the Schoenberg Institute in Los Angeles, just such topics were debated. A variety of opinions was expressed. "The critic should be on the side of the composer," said one composer. But this is to fail to see him as a mediator. Nearer the truth, Ned Rorem commented that "most new music, like most everything, is mediocre and the critic must say so, but let him say so with sorrow, not sarcasm." He must exercise the right to appraise, to esteem or deplore, and his hesitancy or timidity in doing so is what I have suggested to be part of the present crisis.

It may appear to be unnecessary to say, in the words of Leonard Rosenman, one of the composers at the conference, "Criticism must be levied from the standpoint of knowledge of the process of composition"; but this must be said and said loudly, since the number of critics with this kind of competency is small. The model of the music critic is Robert Schumann. The lay person reading Schumann's criticisms of his contemporaries cannot but be impressed, if not awed, by what he soon realizes the composer must have heard in the music he reviewed. He knew what he was hearing, how the music was moving from key to key, and where such movements and arrivals were unconvincing. He lived most of the day and perhaps even the night in a universe of tones, intervals, and keys.

It may be replied, "But things were much easier then." In place of the perpetually changing musical idioms of the present, where one can scarcely regard even the twelve-tone technique as standard for the times, one then had the idiom and system of classical harmony, gradually evolving and mutating, but comparatively easy to teach and learn. On the one hand, however, one must distinguish between the fundamental demands and exigencies of an art of sequenced tones addressed to the ear and, on the other, the particular ways and means that composers adopt to meet those demands and to hold their listeners.[5] We must remind ourselves and the critics of these rather inexorable demands and not accept the flimsy excuse that the particular sounds and their structures appearing in the music of our day are so different from those of Mozart's time that music today is not subject to the same critical demands applicable in the past. This reply would confuse the particular ways of complying with the demands followed at a given time—the binary organization of a movement or a ternary sonata form, for example—with the formal demand itself. The latter derives from the intrinsic temporal nature of music. Now, as then, music still flows on in time, engrossing us either through the satisfaction the ear takes in a presently occurring tone or tone mass, or through the structural development or repetition of musical elements, and it still either fatigues us by its monotony or other formal faults or makes us overcome such physical states and helps the ear eagerly follow where the artist leads.

If the critic, lay or professional, remembers these basic necessities, he will not stand helpless before even the newest offerings. If the artist forgets them, all is lost. He has asked us for ten or twenty minutes or more of our time and he had better make it an interesting experience. He must never forget that he has to fight our fatigue. Think what he must do to keep this at a steady and level state. The quantity or depth of our fatigue inherently tends to increase at the very outset. To counteract this the artist must immediately make things interesting, so interesting that he not only restores us from fatigue to comfortable indifference but beyond this to a heightened interest, which he must maintain to the very end of the time he has asked of us. In this way the curve of our interest will not only be bent to a level, steady state but will in fact be pointed upward. No master of the past or present, writing either in the idiom of classical harmony or of strict serialism or in the very latest tongue has defied this requirement and gotten away with it. From this one can deduce almost all of the structural principles a critic needs to guide him to a judgment that will deserve the respect of the artist as well as the audience.

I mentioned an apparent alternative to the above which should not be overlooked. Fatigue, I think, cannot be ignored, but instead of relying on developing musical structures to counteract it, the artist may defeat it, or try to, by making every present moment so intensely interesting or even so rich and fruity that we are not annoyed by the want of plot or structure in the music and are unaware that we have not departed from somewhere, made our way along a definite path, and then arrived somewhere.

One way or the other, either through the power and attraction of the elements or of the structures, the artist has no alternatives but these, as long as the human ear and body remain what they are.[6] Either the elements of music, the particular tones, intervals, chords, and basic sequences (or if not these, then the pops, gurgles, thumps, swishes, hoots, and honks we have been hearing) are so inherently interesting, beguiling, and magnetic that we forget whether they are or are not arranged in some structurally interesting manner, or they are so well and so strategically ordered that we forget that they themselves may not be very interesting outside such a context.[7]

My point is, if the critic will thoroughly school himself in these basic exigencies of the temporal art of sound, he will be able to be of help to the listener, the layman as well as the professional, and be able also to appraise, to fix for himself and others what he thinks the value of such an effort is. We thus have a sketchy part of an answer to our question about criticism: "Who needs it?" If criticism is what it ought to be, everyone will need it. The composer will need it, since he may need to be told that he has concentrated passionate attention only on the sheer elemental materials he has worked with at the expense of the whole that they constitute, especially the temporal whole, or that he has fallen into the opposite error of wasting great architectonic skill on trivial and intrinsically uninteresting materials that have no real formal relevance toward or attraction for one another. If the layman is not to regard the concert hall only as a place to get an auditory massage, he needs to be given some information about what is being offered to him and what its inner nature and form is. Both of these tasks, as I will show, call not only for explanative but also for appraisive competence. The critic is not just a contributor, but the principal contributor to the task Virgil Thomson assigns him: "explaining the creative or executant artist to the public." But I cannot agree with Thomson that this is not only the main business of critics but "really their *only* business." There comes a time when, as we heard from Ned Rorem, the critic needs to say that the music is mediocre or a failure; or of course he will sometimes say that it is not only an undoubted success with an applauding public, but that it deserves the approbation of those with an intimate acquaintance with the literature of the instrument.

One can sympathize with the composer when he is adversely criticized because he may hear more in the music than anyone else, having seen or heard it grow in his own thought and under his own pen. The work is his and he hears it from his own point of view. If this seems severely circumscribed, one must remember that although the composer is generally no narrowly schooled autodidact, he is under no obligation to have a catholic taste as far as the literature of music or the work of his contemporaries are concerned. Yet this is one of the first requisites for the critic. The artist must assert himself, put himself through as his thought leads him. If he could esteem everything he might have no impulse to affirm his own thought. This, however, leaves us in a curious position. We should show respect to the composer's self-affirmation, perhaps even his self-esteem, but at the same time his self-centered, I do not mean selfish, position makes it difficult for us to take his critical opinion of his own merits as decisive. This eventually leads us toward a paradox that I shall formulate more clearly in a moment.

The kind of criticism I have had in mind here is predicated on an understanding of the demands of the musical medium which the composer dare not ignore. In this respect he can be his own critic and in fact commonly is, and he may be able to correct his own faults. But there is another and altogether different source of criticism that he will be subjected to, and that is criticism in reference to several contexts in which he will find himself, especially comparative criticism that measures his work against other works by his contemporaries and predecessors in the same medium. Here we have criticism in hindsight and in perpetuity of all works that survive in musical consciousness. The context will be ever-changing and absolutely unpredictable. Over this the composer has, of course, no control. He must accept the fact of perpetual critical reassessment. This bespeaks a certain relativism, which is inevitable whenever the artwork is measured, not against what its medium itself demands, but against other works with which the critic sees fit to compare it. The only counsel here must be to arrive at opinions that are well supported in comparison to the works that history has laid before us at a given time.

Such relativistic criticism is fraught with danger, however, one of the more pervasive forms of which is the classification and assimilation of individual artworks under grand rubrics such as the baroque or romanticism or impressionism or other such movements and trends. Art work and artist seem to stand virtually helpless in the face of such assimilation. The art work as it is brought before us, publicated as it were, if it is intended as something to be taken with seriousness, affirms itself alone and asks to be taken on its own merits. Though it may formally appear in a certain genre, such as opera, quartet, musical comedy, lied, or whatever—as such assignable for the convenience of librarians to a certain shelf—it is not long before curators and music directors, and presently art historians and music historians, not only present it under its formal genre, if it has one, but also see it as falling under a type with a different kind of name. It is Gothic, mannerist, baroque, rococo, Augustan, romantic, naturalist, realist, symbolist, or impressionist; it is an example of verismo, cubism, abstract impressionism, op art, pop art, or conceptual art. Except perhaps when they have an application to architecture, it is difficult to offer necessary and sufficient conditions for the use of these terms, because, although they may have some descriptive function, appraisal is intrinsic to their use; and for appraisive terms, no such conditions can be given. (How could one define *Augustan* for example, without the use of appraisive terms? It is also well known that such terms were often first coined and used to discredit certain artworks; for example, *Gothic, mannerist, baroque, romantic, impressionist.*) Appraisal is of course a proper business of the critic, but in being appraised by means of these terms, the artwork is immediately assimilated to other works, and its right to speak for itself is diminished, if not destroyed, at the outset. Although the work may have originated completely innocent of its contemporaries, it is henceforth saddled with a classification, and as time passes it is helpless to resist. It is by now virtually impossible for us to avoid the use of such *historical universals*, as one may call them, but may not the fundamental place they occupy in art history be an error? I do not question the fact that artists have frequently united in sodalities or behind manifestoes, and to that extent they are themselves responsible for their classification. I am asking only why their works must be seen or heard only through the filter of concepts whose provenance may lie far afield from them.

But this is only one side of the matter. On the other, we must ask what the implications would be for criticism if we were to free the artist from the jurisdiction of the apparently alien tribunal of these and other classifying concepts and respect only his own judgment of himself and his work. You can now see the emerging shape of the paradox I spoke of. Can we either accept or reject the artist's estimate of himself? Can we either accept or reject the judgments of art history that see artworks as falling into contexts and involve their assimilation under historical universals?

Let me try to present the issues as clearly as possible. The artwork comes to us affirming itself alone and demanding to be judged on its own merits, but history plays a trick on it by revealing it almost immediately to lie within several contexts, the foremost of these being other artworks with which it is inevitably compared and to which it is as inevitably assimilated.[8] The problem then is that if we judge it with reference to other works, the standards it must live up to are set by these others and may be alien to it. By this procedure its individuality is compromised or at least not respected. On the other hand, no work can pretend to be judged by standards it erects for itself, since the very notion of such ad hoc standards is meaningless. We have then the uncomfortable situation in which either the artist becomes his own critic—a role he is generally not qualified for—or the work is judged by standards derived from a wholly different inspiration. If there is no third way out, we either surrender to the artist, and then criticism is at an end because there are as many criteria as artworks, or we surrender to the art historians, who will tend to deal with artworks only as members of classes. We cannot accept either of these solutions, nor can we accept their contraries: we cannot altogether accept or condemn art and music history wholesale or the artist's self-affirmation.

I have already suggested a solution to these problems: we must remember what the requirements of the time-medium that the composer adopts are; they alone transcend him. Since he has chosen this medium, he has submitted himself to its demands. These demands alone can give the critic or historian a basis for judging artworks, at the same time enabling him to offer constructive help both to the artist and his audience. Much more needs to be said to defend this way of legitimizing the occupation of the critic, but perhaps enough has been said so that we can turn next to the craft of the critic.

The Craft of Criticism

We must now consider more closely how criticism and, in particular, music criticism works in order to come to some conclusions about how it is to be used and how it may be misused.

The most familiar and in the end the most fundamental critical concept is of course *the good*, together with its various near-synonyms and negations. Although this concept is involved in all characterizing appraisal, it is not of overwhelming significance when spoken by itself and, then, possesses little or no material content. Although the good is both the end and culmination of the appraisive process and is involved in all subordinate appraisive concepts, its material support must come from somewhere outside itself. That is, if I say "A is good," I have essentially offered only the promise of being able to support this by a particular characterization of A, that which is being criticized or appraised, which I shall call the *subject*. If sometimes we want to be drastic and say "it's just no good," or "he's no good," what we are saying is that there is no relevant characterization of a crediting nature we can offer in favor of such a subject. But we cannot just leave matters there, for by itself 'good' or 'bad' is only the promise of a materially significant appraisal, not a realization of one.

In general, remarks using the familiar idiom *good* may be called *commendations*, while those that we are obliged to furnish in support of them may be called *characterizations*. Commendations are incapable of either truth or falsity, and characterizations are capable of one or the other only in a limited sense, as I shall explain presently. Suppose I have occasion to discommend someone with a term such as *bad*. I may support this by saying that the person is persistently sullen or insolent or, even worse, that he is dishonest. Again, I may regard some musical subject as strident and cacophonous, or as being artificial, "bloodless, paper music." In these cases I think it is an error to suppose that such remarks are either objectively true or false; rather, they are either apt characterizations of the subject or they are not. The characterization "bloodless, paper music," made by a critic in New York earlier in this century about Schoenberg, is neither true nor false.

To take another example, I once attended a concert with a friend at which two pieces, easy to compare, one by Debussy and the other by Schoenberg, appeared on the program. We discussed them a bit afterwards. The Schoenberg, said he, seemed to him *"gemacht,"* that is, artificial, lifeless, smelling of the lamp. (I may remark in passing that my friend was a scholar of French music and wore the emblem of the Legion of Honor in his lapel.) I think you may agree that *gemacht* can be an apt characterization, if not of Schoenberg's music, then of a work of someone else you are acquainted with.

Or let me quote characterizations such as the following. Characterizing Verdi's *Requiem* Virgil Thomson says, "it is gaudy, surprising, sumptuous, melodramatic, and grand . . . a sincere piece of theatrical Italian Catholicism." Pevsner, offering several highly condensed characterizations, says "there is luxuriant beauty in Titian, stately gravity in Raphael and gigantic strength in Michelangelo, but mannerist types are slim, elegant, and of a stiff and highly self-conscious deportment." These are apt and telling characterizations, whether we agree with them or not, but they are neither true nor false. Although all of them may be based on real properties of their subjects, they do not reveal facts about the artists or their works as expressed in statements intended to be taken as true. If a critic tells us that the architecture of mannerism was inferior to that of the High Renaissance, he may be able to support it by characterizing typical examples of the two, but there is no fact that reads "the architecture of mannerism is inferior to that of the High Renaissance," as there is that St. Peter's in Rome is larger than St. Paul's in London. All hankering after eternally true aesthetic judgments is idle and represents a misunderstanding of what is said in such so-called judgments.

We can develop this idea somewhat further by observing that commendations and characterizations are not detachable, as one might say, from the speaker.[9] It is always relevant to ask who has appraised some subject in a given fashion. But statements that are confirmed as true, although they may be uttered by some speaker and although the facts may have been discovered by some particular person, do not depend on such persons in any way. Facts are discovered, found, turned up, but they are not invented by speakers in order to express their responses or their feelings toward subjects. It should further be observed that a factual statement, if confirmed or demonstrated as true, is detachable not only from him who utters or discovers it, but from the evidence on which it is based. We may, of course, want to know what the evidence is, but if the factual statement follows from the evidence, that is logically the end of the matter.[10]

The foregoing has, however, an awkward unavoidable consequence, which will be recognized as one of circularity. Factual statements are directed *ad rem*, toward the facts they express. But appraisive statements are always tied to their speakers, *ad hominem*. Hence we seem to have to take them on the authority of who utters them. Quite often we do so very frankly. We are more inclined to listen to the critic of a leading newspaper or journal than to a barber or busdriver when we want to hear an opinion on music. (The critic-barber segregation refers only to the probable degree of acquaintance with music that they have.) Thus, we tend to place our reliance on the critic because of his knowledge of music, but we rely on his knowledge of music, rather than some other person's, because he is a critic or he is the critic so-and-so. It is the same with moral opinions. I may rely on so-and-so's moral advice because of who he is and what I think his character is, but I may base what I think of his character on the kind of moral advice he has given. The only way to accommodate oneself to this, which is so typical of moral and other appraisive situations, is to work in both directions, testing one of these by the other in numerous cases until one is satisfied that the critic deserves our reliance. There is scarcely any other way out of this logical trap; one merely adjusts himself to being caught in it.

But there is one more, and indeed more important, fact about the situation that places matters in a somewhat different light. Although critical judgments are irremediably *ad hominem* in character, the *homo* in the situation may be myself alone, that is, when my own opinions are referred back to me alone. This is the most typical situation. We now have only ourselves to rely upon, and our appraisal depends upon how extensive our command of the vocabulary of appraisal is and upon our knowledge of the subject matter in question. The characterizations we now make are in fact the originals of appraisal, that is, the ultimate foundation of our lives as beings that appraise, judge, and evaluate as well as register or take note of facts.[11] They are the appraisive analogues of reports of our sense impressions and enjoy a unique kind of authority. If you think I am snobbish, insolent, stingy, or selfish (or, as I hope, the opposite of these), or if you think that the music is colorless, diffuse, or depressing, or that it is delicate, disciplined, or vivid, we may assume that you feel that way about me or the music, although these characterizations generally appraise us of much more than feelings, as we shall see. You should in general be able to point to particular actions of mine or to particular aspects of the music, to clarify just what you are characterizing in me or in the music with these words. In the end, some appraisive terms will serve as vehicles through which you convey or express your response, and these betoken what I have called the originals of appraisal.

The fact is, I have managed to get something out into the public domain by using

words and thus concepts. The reduction so often undertaken by some moral philosophers of all appraisal to feelings, to "a sentiment of praise or blame," as Hume said,
utterly local to the individual, completely neglects the fact that when I speak ill of
you, I do not just want to inform you of my feelings (which you may cheerfully
choose to ignore, and rightly so), but rather, I want you to attend to something
about yourself that prompts my negative feelings. And if I have aptly characterized
you, something has been presented to you that you can confirm (or disconfirm) by
self-examination, something public and conceptually communicable by means of
which I have, as the current phrase goes, gotten through to you in a way in which
mere spasms of positive or negative emotion toward you may not. You will now, in
hearing me, apply what I have said to yourself, and if this is, let us say, highly dis-
crediting (e.g., *insolent*, *selfish*) you cannot help responding with a certain shock,
because we do not normally inculpate ourselves in such terms. To get the point, the
message, you must suffer this initial shock, or else you have not understood me at all.
After that moment, which may or may not prolong itself, you may see the point of
my charge: if you do, you may regret your actions, you may even be penitent.

One must be sure to notice in the foregoing discussion that something conceptual
is conveyed in our appraisals and characterizations of each other in addition to what
is generally considered to be a feeling of some sort. This conceptual component of all
genuine characterizations is present in all moral or personal criticism and in the
criticism of artists and their art. This component is what I said might, in a limited
sense, be regarded as having a reference to truth or falsity since it identifies the
subject or the particular aspect of the subject that is being appraised. Besides this,
there is also the appraisive component, which signifies that that subject is not a
matter of indifference to the appraiser, that he may even feel strongly about him or
her or it. The feeling is not itself the appraisal but merely accompanies or at most
betokens it. Many appraisals and references to good or bad are very commonly
suffused with emotion, and many are not.

If the preceding sounds as if it is concerned mostly with moral matters, its
application to criticism can easily be shown also. Since, as I said at the outset, I am
keeping my mind particularly on criticism contemporary with the composer, the
application should be clear. The vocabulary of critics, particularly in the press and
periodicals but also in the more academic analyses of musicologists, includes not just
good and *bad*, but a mass of critical terms and phrases that is extensive and is
constantly being augmented, from metaphor, for example. The composer is unlikely
to be impressed by someone's merely saying his work is good or bad without
supporting this assertion with specific characterizations of his music, nor by someone's merely saying he likes or does not like the music, unless it is someone whose
opinion he is inclined to honor (raising the *ad hominem* problem of circularity
mentioned previously). And if the critic seems to be merely venting his emotion, the
composer can even say without insolence, You may keep your emotions and dislikes
to yourself. What alone ought to impress the composer is the reference to his own
practice by the descriptive component of the characterization of his music, that is,
its conceptual content rather than the emotional force of it. Even in unfavorable

characterization the critic and the recipient of criticism can agree on a true statement about what they are responding to in the subject of appraisal. So, for example, they can agree that what one of them appraises as fussy and trivial is precisely what the other appraises as subtle and delicate; or, in the moral situation, that what one person regards as insulting and insolent is precisely what the other regards as fearless and frank; or, in a still more forceful example, in a child-beating case, the very same action or result of action may be characterized as aggression or again as disciplinary. The *what* in each of these cases can receive a neutral description that is either true or false.

We must now attend a little more closely to the apprehension of just what it is in these subjects of appraisal that is being appraised; just what properties are the actual target of characterization. In criticism of music, appraisive terms perform their function properly only when there is a reference, confirmable as true or false, to the real properties of the subject appraised. If this reference is missing, the term is merely one of abuse or an enthusiastic puff. The common vernacular, slang, and obscenities provide numerous examples of such abusives. Proper appraisives, on the other hand, draw attention to some feature of the subject and are not simply emotional outbursts for or against it. Hence, a good critic can almost be defined as someone who has the perceptiveness and the conceptual ability to bring to light in the subject traits that had escaped us but of whose reality we are convinced, once we grasp them. One might call this the *descriptive function of appraisive terms*, since the reference is to properties of the subject that are in principle capable of description, earlier referred to as their descriptive component.

To illustrate this point I will not attempt to coin a startlingly apt new characterization, since I am not a critic. But a few familiar examples will be just as effective, drawn from criticism directed toward the elemental qualities or structure or style or other functional aspects of artworks: *lucid* and *muddy*, *florid* and *gaunt*, *inevitable* and *obvious*, *organic* and *mechanical*, *luxuriant* and *sombre*, *generous* and *prolix*, *tender* and *brusque*, *frigid* and *dead*. Some of these words, which are not only familiar but even trite, may nonetheless be effective. Some of the most surprisingly effective appraisives are those that cross over from one medium to another. *Lucid*, *muddy*, and *florid*, drawn from vision, may be applied to music; *generous*, *brusque*, or *dead*, drawn from the realm of living things, and abstractions like *organic*, *mechanical*, *obvious*, *inevitable*, and *prolix* are applied to any of the arts. All of them could be and have been used by critics to draw our attention to something in music or the other arts which in listening to or watching we may have overlooked. Each of them has a certain limited but inherent descriptive power, although its intent as a whole is appraisive.[12] This selective descriptive power may enable us, when we find the critic applying it to music, to hear something we might not hear unaided by the term. To hear music equipped with a generous fund of critical concepts is to realize it as a genuine value experience. To hear it uncritically, unequipped with a power of discriminating its inner quality, is to enjoy only a warm musical shower. The proper hearing of music is inherently critical. The critic is the ideal listener. Whatever his shortcomings, he is necessary to the life and advancement of music. He must not abandon his appraisive function for any of the flimsy reasons that have been offered recently. This, then, may help us answer the question about the need for criticism.

We should rejoice that it can be said of music, perhaps more than of any other art, that it has something for everyone. If I have been a bit patronizing about uncritical listeners, I concede that in the end it is important to invite all persons into the world of musical culture, to bring them in as participants at whatever level they have the capacity to function. I do not think any participation at any level is wholly passive. I find the lofty attitudes of Thomson and others not easy to endure; such critics seem not to care a fig for the musical culture of people as a whole. But in fact, most people are willing to yield the judgment on those vast reaches of the musical realm they cannot or cannot as yet share in to the experts. Even journalistic criticism can be defended, I think, since it may in the end awaken critical capacities and attitudes in the listening participants. Without this, music becomes either only a pleasant massage or a trying, if not painful, experience.

The Malpractice of Criticism

There is much more that can be said on the subjects we have taken up. If I have been able to offer a defense of criticism, it has certainly not been on behalf of the efforts of musical Monday morning quarterbacks only but *a fortiori* of the more scholarly efforts the layman generally does not consult. It is safe to say that, although musical analysis does not in general casually scatter abroad a mass of emotively charged characterizations, it nevertheless reveals its critical intent even if it speaks only of the structure of musical works in seemingly objective terms. For even in this case it will be concerned among other things with the coherence of works, the relevance of their parts to one another, and their culminations and climaxes, all of which are or use essentially characterizing concepts.

All critical concourse with such a phenomenon as music, or any of the other arts and much else besides, is inherently appraisive. As one might expect, criticism is also subject, like all human efforts, to a certain pathology. In trying to define the proper occupation of the critic in the foregoing, I have already either said or implied a great deal about critical pathology or malpractice, if the terms are not too strong. I will draw specific attention to a few more of the kinds of errors the critical profession can succumb to and, if I am not altogether mistaken, may recently have been succumbing to.

First, the critic or analyst may substitute description for appraisal. It is, of course, a very important part of the critic's job that he explain the creative or executant artist to the public. He should, however, remember that as an explicator he would be only a kind of assistant impresario who manages to clear the obstacles in the way of the audience's view of the stage and what transpires on it. His error would be in thinking that this is criticism. As we have seen, critical characterization is inherently and indefeasibly appraisive, and there is no way to renounce the "judicial" element in criticism, as some aestheticians have demanded.

A recent variant of the error in question is a little more serious; it shows a certain abdication by the critic of his appraisive duties. One whose attention is finely focused will surely have run across this often in discussions by critics of the works of visual arts especially, but also of musical compositions and performances. For this one needs attention that is a little more keenly attuned to exactly what is being said than the average reader devotes to such matters. The critic, baffled by what he sees or hears, unable to find anything in the critical tradition that would seem to bear on the novelty before him, too timid forthrightly to appraise the work perhaps adversely, and afraid to repudiate the new or to discourage the artist, who might find it "hard going," falls into the habit of offering only a kind of paraphrase of the work. This may vaguely sound like what has been called characterization, but it is not, although in particular cases the line may be hard to draw between the two. Confronted by utterly novel uses of materials, of paper, steel, wire, plastics, glass, textiles, wood, concrete, stone, leather, string, and much more in unusual forms, or by materials never before offered as music, the critic seems to wish to convey to us in words what he has before him. If he merely wants us to have a bare notion of what is being offered for display or listening, this may suffice. But we will all catch on much better if we simply go and look at it or listen to it. As against paraphrase, one picture is worth a thousand words and one glance is even better. This species of talk may have a certain use, but it is not criticism. When, on the other hand, we say in a manner to credit or discredit that certain colors are warm, cool, glowing, dead, sombre, harsh, or livid; that lines are florid, resilient, nerveless, dull, hard, or mechanical; that tones are luxuriant, warm, strident, fierce, rude, taxing, yelping, jagged, or bloodless, we are offering criticism of a very elemental sort. These are examples of what must be distinguished from mere paraphrases.

Let me illustrate descriptive paraphrasing a little more concretely by referring to some examples that are typical of many critical notices or reviews of visual works currently appearing in galleries. In the work of a sculptor, as observed by an art critic, there appear "a couple of long, vertical sandwiches of timbers under glass, held in place by steel clamps at top and bottom, that one remembers from [the artist's] previous exhibit. There follows a pair of thinner wall pieces in which the curve is introduced—its first appearance in [his] works since the visionary reliquaries he used to make these many years ago—in the form of a thin rounded plane protruding from between parts of thin, vertical upright planks." The article continues with more of such description, which is of minimal use to readers who have not seen the exhibit, and still less to those who have. In concluding that some work's "appearance of highly compressed energy is thoroughly convincing," a slight touch of appraisal, "convincing," whatever this may mean, rounds off the notice. We may well ask why space is devoted to such a doubtful exercise of acute powers of observation. Who needs this?

The critic then continues with a similar description of another artist's work.

> Her concrete material is ordinary sewing thread—hundreds of lengths
> of it—with which she has fashioned two constructions of environ-

[111]

mental dimensions. . . . One [construction] in black thread consists of three pairs of troughlike shapes, one above the other, formed by running long horizontal strands from a windowsill to virtually invisible nylon guy cords on the other side of the room, then gracefully draping multitudes of shorter strands at regular intervals across the larger threads. [Another construction] in whitish threads, is a horizontal lattice-like grid, suspended several inches above head level from which hundreds of verticals fall loosely toward the floor.

In appearance, both works are primarily spindly spider-web-like drawings in space but, almost subversively, they also assume distinctly sculptural properties. The latter piece, which dissolves almost to invisibility in the light of a window behind it, is particularly provocative, projecting a nearly territorial sense of space into which one is loathe to intrude, no doubt at least in part because of the fragility of the construction.

Indeed, there is an intimidating, don't come too close presence to both these pieces that totally belies their graceful, gossamer appearance, in delicacy there is strength. And so [the] work is far less forthright than it first appears.[13]

We may well ask why "territorial sense of space" is not a redundancy and observe the far-fetched if not indecodable metaphors "subversively" and "intimidating." But apart from this, since the critic does not employ his visual acumen to offer us and the artist an apt characterization of the work, his effort comes to naught: we do not need mere description, and even if we could use it, its point is lost when we have to grope blindly to see the connection between the few words that have a kind of characterizing air and all the description that has gone before. But many journalistic art critiques are far worse than this.

The touches of appraisal in these reviews are confined to the terms *provocative*, *intimidating*, and *convincing*. These are elicitive appraisive terms, the weakest a critic can use, since they tell us nothing about the subject appraised except that it has a disposition to elicit a given response in the observer or critic. It is easy to find reviews of music that are of a similar orientation.

A second dysfunction of criticism reveals itself in the critic's failure of nerve in the face of the novelty in the extremest sense of current works, so novel that one must seriously consider whether the new works may not be music at all, not sculpture at all, and in the end, not art at all. Sometimes such things need to be said, but we would be better off it we could use the terms in no invidious sense. It is true that new art mediums are invented from time to time, and it is altogether possible that something should in the future take the place of art without being art at all. But even all of the familiar media had to be invented at some time or other, and older ones have often survived alongside them. Religion has survived even though some of its functions have been taken over by the arts. In the past, in a narrower sphere, it has occurred that what was put forth as poetry was declared not poetry at all, not art at all. There have been many degrees of this.[14]

Even if we think something is "not music at all," it may nevertheless deserve to be heard and to be appraised. We should not let the mere word or classification *art* or *music* stand between us and the work or impede the opportunity to hear or see it.

We must distinguish between saying that something may fall far afield of what has been regarded as music and limiting the opportunities to attend to it. The present state is one where, fortunately, we have numerous different musical enterprises, some of which are music only in a dubious sense. Perhaps we are approaching the situation in which the term *music* is itself used in a completely nonappraisive sense. But the important point is that the works are still subject to characterization and appraisal in accordance with the demands of their mediums.

It is important that critics examine all works in as severe and searching a way as older works have been examined. It does not really advance the new music to treat it as too fragile to be subjected to thoroughgoing criticism. If it is put forth as music it should be judged as such. And since it is now being heard in the context of the older music, it is always possible that it may or may not be an advance over the old. What people were beginning to hear in concert rooms and opera houses about 1800 or 1810 soon made them wonder, and then doubt, whether sun and moon would forever rise and set on Mozart, Haydn, and dozens of minor figures writing in a similar idiom. What is necessary in a time and place like ours is not that every novelty be praised but that it be heard and its value carefully discriminated. I think failure to provide resolute criticism is a serious error.

A third error of criticism manifests itself in the failure of the critic to command a full range of the conceptual resources of criticism and how they are interrelated. The cause of this failure I will suggest in a moment. I shall not expound this error in detail, but an example or two may make things sufficiently clear. For purposes of the argument, let us conjure up a critic whom we will present as somewhat more one-sided than any we would normally encounter. This critic uniformly favors music in which he finds commendable values expressible in such terms as *intelligible, lucid, vivid, perspicuous; logical, well planned, possessing a sturdy framework; consistent, organic, a whole;* and of course, *unity*, which is the flag under which all of these sail (quadrant I in figure 1). It is easy to guess what terms he would use when rejecting what he hears: *confused, blurred, obscure, loosely sprawling, not well integrated, diffuse, disjointed, shapeless,* and of course, *chaos* and *chaotic* as the vice typifying the whole class (quadrant III). These are his favorite virtues and vices, and when it comes to formal and structural considerations, these are what he hopes for or abhors. So attached may he become to these that he finds few or no occasions in which he must express himself in terms such as *overorganized, obvious,* and *predictable* (quadrant IV). And since he finds no need for these vices, neither are the following virtues for him: *dense, elaborate, florid, multifaceted, rich in detail; difficult* and *profound;* he has little use for the basic virtue in this class, *variety* (quadrant II). He likes things to be neat and tidy. For him there are really no alternatives to his favorite virtues and vices, and that is the source of his malpractice. The logical alternative to his lucidity may be profundity, but for him this is only obscurity. Similarly he is loath to admit that there can be too much of perspicuity, organicity, or unity.

Turning in a different direction, another kind of critic may invoke only the opposite or alternative virtues and vices. For him only what is varied, complex, rich, or even difficult is valuable; all else is monotonous, obvious, or predictable. Neither

FIGURE 1

I Unity	II Variety
intelligible lucid perspicuous vivid	dense elaborate florid multifaceted rich in detail
logical possessing a sturdy framework well planned	difficult profound
consistent organic a whole	
IV Monotony	III Chaos, chaotic
obvious overorganized predictable	blurred confused diffuse disjointed loosely sprawling obscure not well integrated shapeless

of these critics recognizes that there may be virtues corresponding to what he regards as vices, as unity might be said to be a successful, tolerable, or desirable monotony, and variety a desirable form of chaos, if I may exaggerate to make a point.

By looking to the pairings of virtues and vices, both aesthetic and moral, that a critic favors, one can soon find some of the unmistakable traits of what we may call the inflexible critical personality, such as that of the critic in question. Earlier I offered to exempt the creative artist from the obligation to be appreciative of all the visions and revelations that other artists in his own artistic genre have had. But we cannot similarly exempt the critic. The inflexible critic is as great a menace as the permissive critic: it is difficult to say which of them can do more harm. There are, of course, psychic causes for such inflexibility which I cannot explore now; rather it is more important for the reader to be able to identify such personalities.

Let us take another example of inflexibility in the critic. Figure 2 presents a stock of critical concepts arranged in a manner similar to figure 1. Consider now critics who incline markedly either toward I and III or toward II and IV in their choice of concepts of value. The first kind of critic will neglect to think that there is a vice that subjects may fall into that contrasts with what he is inclined to praise in terms such as those in I; that is, instead of being readily thought to be elegant, graceful, or exquisite, subjects ought to be scrutinized closely to see that they are not manneristic, affected, trifling, or frivolous. Or again, some other critic likes only works of grand, monumental, or powerful character (II), neglecting to discriminate these

FIGURE 2

I	delicate	II	austerity
	elegant		grand, grandeur
	exquisite		gravity
	grace		monumental
	refined		splendor
	suave		stability
			sublime

			energy
			power
			virility

IV	affected	III	cold
	frippery		banality
	frivolous		bombastic
	mannerism		frigid
	mesquinerie		megalomania
	pettiness		pompous
	trifling, trivial		ponderous
			pretentious

			coarse
			convulsive
			crude
			savage
			violent

clearly from those that are cold, pompous, and banal, or violent and convulsive (III). Since so many classes of appraisives fall naturally into this fourfold arrangement, one can easily identify still other types of narrow or inflexible critics or criticism.

It should be added that since moral characterizations similarly fall into a fourfold order, inflexible personalities are found in that domain as well, and indeed far more often. Similarly, their value vocabulary helps us to identify these personalities.

The fourth, and perhaps the most important among the critical shortcomings of the present time is the failure or neglect, in the face of the newest and most bizarre presentations, to judge what is put forward as music, especially instrumental music, as an art in which success must derive from either of two ultimate sources: (1) the attraction, charm, magnetism, or satisfaction for the ear in the least structural elements of music which on familiar instruments I would say must be the intervals (even more fundamentally than tones) and (2) the large- or small-scale bearing, trends, tensions, and tendencies that the ear discerns in these intervals and tones toward one another. If alternative smallest elements originating in various kinds of clang and noise producers are employed, the composer has undertaken a job of extraordinary difficulty, since the bearings here are of infinite variety. They must however be made clear to the listener. Music in the traditional manner can always fall back on the intrinsic charm or attraction of the tones when their bearings on one another are obscure or far-fetched. With the newer alternative modes a burden is placed on the elemental noises that they can carry, if at all, only with difficulty. The reason, then, for the listener's bewilderment or even hostility is that he can take little satisfaction in the elements and cannot grasp their presumptive bearing on one another. The reason for the satisfaction the public continues to take in music in the older idiom is that the medium affords satisfaction on both counts.

Many critics are often seemingly unable to cope with this situation. Under the great circus tent of music one can gather many things, even noises, seeing that in limited measure they have been present in music as far back as the memory of man reaches. But music, old or new, must always occupy a time both elapsed and filled from a beginning to an end, and if the critic fails to demand that the music justify its occupying this stretch of time; if he fails to observe that the time is filled with nothing and that it has not justified this vacuum in some convincing way; if, failing to discern any bearing of the elements on one another, he fails to notice that elements are actually of no intrinsic elemental interest; if, as has so often happened recently, the composer regales the audience with mirror-image identical elements, monotonously repeated, and the critic simply fails to register boredom, I would say he has failed altogether as a critic. It is an unfailing mark of a critic worthy of the name to know when to be bored, and to say so.[15]

Notes

1. Karl Aschenbrenner, *The Concepts of Criticism* (Boston: Reidel, Dordrecht: 1974), especially the "Critical Source Book," pp. 343-536.

2. Attention must also be drawn to the inevitable and perpetual revaluation to which artworks are subject in the course of time.

3. See a report by Michael Walsh in the San Francisco *Chronicle*, 6 August 1978, of a conference of critics and composers at the Schoenberg Institute of the University of Southern California, Los Angeles. Quotations below of remarks by Virgil Thomson, Ned Rorem, and Leonard Rosenman are taken from the same article.

4. What can one say but that a contemporary artist like Pierre Boulez fears the competition he has to face from the masters of the past when he says, "It is not enough to deface the Mona Lisa because.that does not kill the Mona Lisa. All the art of the past must be destroyed" (*New York Times* interview, 20 June 1971). This should be regarded as an encouragement to vandalism; nor is he the only one who has spoken in such inflammatory terms.

5. Cf. Roger Sessions's remarks on the use of the word *form*: "'Form' is too often conceived in terms of 'forms' . . . frozen from the distant past. . . . All too seldom is it conceived as an outgrowth of musical ideas themselves, in their immediate and dynamic aspects." "To the Editor," in *Perspectives on American Composers*, ed. Benjamin Boretz and Edward T. Cone (New York: Norton, 1971), p. 108.

6. We must content ourselves in English with abstractions such as *interesting*, *magnetic* to designate the attraction that musical elements, tones or intervals, exert on us and the satisfaction we take in them, some more than others. Compare the German *Reiz* or the Hungarian *vonzo*, two very apt terms for this.

7. Essentially we must regard intervals, not tones, as the real elements of music. A given tone may have an unmistakable quality, but it must also be recognized as being what it is. If you sound middle C on the piano for me today and tomorrow the adjacent D-flat, I will probably not be able to tell you whether the two tones are different or the same since they differ only in pitch but hardly in character. Each of the twelve intervals in the octave, however, has a definite character of its own. Simultaneously or in sequence, intervals make music as we have known it possible. Indeed, all Western music, with rare and mostly recent exceptions, is constructed with just these twelve.

8. Another kind of context is the whole extent of the artist's life. When his works are said to be the work of youth, maturity, or old age, they are being regarded as occupying a certain place in the whole context of a lifetime.

9. Karl Aschenbrenner, "Artistic Disclosure," *Studia Estetyczne* (Warsaw) 4 (1967): 283-93.

10. The qualifications that need to be made to this, which concern the nature of explanation and theory construction, are irrelevant to the subject matter under discussion here.

11. It is almost inevitable that we will refer to our appraisals as judgments. But if we do, we should take care to remember that when we characterize artworks, we are not judging in accordance with rules. There are no rules for aesthetic appraisal or characterization: what we need is keen insight into the nature of the object appraised and a resource of appraisive concepts liberal enough to enable us to offer an apt characterization of it. Moral appraisal, on the other hand, is judgment and is directed toward human actions as falling under types and classes such as personal offenses, torts, misdemeanors, or crimes. Thus, judgments are referrable to rules governing such classes of actions. As noted earlier, we must always seek to do justice to the sheer individuality of artworks. New artworks are not just more specimens of some previously established class or type, like plums that are essentially the same from year to year. Rather, they are like new *species*, something which the organic world rarely produces.

12. The appraisive component stamps its own character on the appraisive concept or sentence as a whole, even though in a limited sense truth and falsity apply to the descriptive aspect or component of the sentence. It is something like multiplying a positive number by a negative, if we think of the descriptive aspect as corresponding to a positive and the appraisive to a negative number: e.g., $2 \times -2 = -4$.

13. San Francisco *Chronicle*, 1 October 1977.

14. Cf. discussion of the use of certain terms as appraisive in what may be called an "eminent" sense in Aschenbrenner's *Concepts of Criticism*, pp. 329-32. This is what is involved in phrases such as "not art, or music, at all."

15. One could wish that all music critics would retain and cultivate their capacity for boredom as well as Heuwel Tircuit has. Subjected in a concert of newer composers to "little chips of simplistic materials . . . played again and again perhaps hundreds or thousands of times," he responds by saying that although this "may delight the unknowledgeable, [it] cannot but make the judicious grieve and yawn." Judging from numerous other responses, his capacity appears to amount to an enviable talent for the selective boredom that so many other critics lack (see San Francisco *Chronicle*, 5 October 1976).